Learning English with the Bible

TEXTBOOK

BY
LOUISE M. EBNER

AMG
PUBLISHERS

Learning English with the Bible

TEXTBOOK

A SYSTEMATIC APPROACH TO
BIBLE-BASED ENGLISH GRAMMAR

BY
LOUISE M. EBNER

JOHN 20:31

"BUT THESE ARE WRITTEN, THAT YE MIGHT BELIEVE THAT JESUS IS THE CHRIST, THE SON OF GOD; AND THAT BELIEVING YE MIGHT HAVE LIFE THROUGH HIS NAME."

LEARNING ENGLISH WITH THE BIBLE
TEXTBOOK

Published by AMG Publishers

Ninth Printing, 2002

ISBN 0-89957-565-X

Printed in the United States of America
07 06 05 04 03 02 –RO– 14 13 12 11 10 9

INTRODUCTION

The Bible is God-inspired. Every word in the original manuscripts of the canonical books of the Old and New Testaments were selected by God and given to the writer to give to us with the preservation of his own individual style. That is a miracle.

Since the Bible is such a miraculous book, why is it not used in classrooms as a perfect language instrument? The world is poorer for not having used the Bible also for grammatical and systematical purposes.

God has given Mrs. Louise Ebner, a veteran educator, the vision to use God's Word, the Word not only for salvation and inspiration but also for linguistic instruction.

Of what use is knowing grammar if one's life is not in conformity with the creator's designs?

It is our hope that as grammar is learned through God's Word, that Word will sink into the heart while the mind is instructed.

Spiros Zodhiates, Th.D.
President, AMG International

TABLE OF CONTENTS

PART I
LEARNING PARTS OF SPEECH

PART II
USING PARTS OF SPEECH

PART III
VERBALS

PART IV
SENTENCE STRUCTURE

SUGGESTIONS FOR COMPOSITION

Exercises entitled **"EXPLORING TRUTHS"** are found at the end of chapters.

PART I

PARTS OF SPEECH

One important function of grammar is the study of the eight basic parts of speech. Every word in the English language may be classified according to its special function in a sentence as one of the eight parts of speech:

- **NOUN**
- **VERB**
- **ADJECTIVE**
- **CONJUNCTION**
- **PRONOUN**
- **ADVERB**
- **PREPOSITION**
- **INTERJECTION**

This study of grammar begins with the noun and its function.

CHAPTER 1

LEARNING ABOUT NOUNS

LESSON 1-A RECOGNITION OF NOUNS

- A *noun* is the name of a person, place, thing, idea or quality.

Examples:

a. person	God, baby, Moses, creator, assembly
b. place	garden, heaven, Jerusalem, home
c. thing	ark, tree, candlestick, rod, ship
d. idea or quality	freedom, love, peace, joy, faith

EXERCISE 1

Underline every noun in the following sentences.

1. Now when Jesus was born in Bethlehem of Judaea in the days of Herod the king, behold, there came wise men from the east to Jerusalem, saying, "Where is he that is born King of the Jews?"
2. "For we have seen his star in the east, and are come to worship him."
3. When Herod the king heard these things, he was troubled, and all Jerusalem with him.
4. And when he had gathered all the chief priests and scribes of the people together, he demanded of them where Christ should be born.
5. And they said unto him, "In Bethlehem of Judaea: for thus it is written by the prophet, 'And you Bethlehem, in the land of Judaea are not the least among the princes of Judah, for out of you shall come a Governor that shall rule my people Israel'."

from Matthew 2:1–6

EXERCISE 2

In the space provided write a definition of a noun.

EXERCISE 3

List ten persons found in the Bible.

EXERCISE 4

List ten places found in the Bible.

EXERCISE 5

List ten things mentioned in the Bible.

EXERCISE 6

List ten ideas suggested by Biblical stories. (Example: Obedience — Noah built an ark.)

EXPLORING TRUTHS

Consider the ten persons, places, things, and ideas which you discovered. Do you believe that God has a purpose for every detail placed in His Word? Ask God what lessons He has for you in the people, places, things or ideas which you have listed.

LESSON 1-B KINDS OF NOUNS

There are several different kinds of *nouns:*

- A *common noun* is the name that is applied in common to all the members of a group of persons, places, things, or ideas. Common nouns are not generally capitalized.
- A *proper noun* is the name applied to particular or specific persons, places, things or ideas. Proper nouns are capitalized.
- A *collective noun* is the name applied to a group or class considered as a unit.
- A *concrete noun* is the name applied to something that can be perceived by one or more of the senses.
- An *abstract noun* is the name applied to a quality or general idea.

Examples:

a. common noun	man, woman, river, grass, book.
b. proper noun	Adam, Eve, Euphrates River, Bible, Battle of Armagedon.
c. collective noun	herd, flock, crowd, group.
d. concrete noun	water, perfume, honey, flower, satin.
e. abstract noun	bravery, anger, pity, ambition, courage.

EXERCISE 7

Underline the nouns in the following sentences and write CM over each common noun, PR over each proper noun, CN over each concrete noun, CL over each collective noun, and AB over each abstract noun. (Sometimes a noun may fit into one or more kinds of nouns.)

1. Then Herod, when he had privily called the wise men, enquired of them diligently what time the star appeared.
2. And sent them to Bethlehem and said, "Go and search diligently for the young child; and when you have found him, bring me word again that I may come and worship him also."
3. When they had heard the king, they departed; and lo, the star, which they saw in the east, went before them till it came and stood over where the young child was.
4. When the group of wise men saw the star, they rejoiced with exceeding great joy.

from Matthew 2:7–10

EXERCISE 8

List as many proper nouns for God as you can find in the Bible.
Example: Jehovah

EXERCISE 9

List as many common nouns as you can to show a characteristic of God.
Example: refuge

EXPLORING TRUTHS

Do you believe that God is the same yesterday, today, and forever? Can you appropriate one of the meanings of the names of God into your life?

TEST ON NOUNS

Underline the nouns in the following passage.

The proverbs of Solomon, the son of David, king of Israel:

> To know wisdom and instruction; to perceive the words of understanding;
>
> To receive the instruction of wisdom, justice, judgment and equity;
>
> To give subtility to the simple, to the young man knowledge and discretion.
>
> A wise man will hear, and will increase learning; and a man of understanding shall attain unto wise counsels.
>
> To understand a proverb and the interpretation; the words of the wise and their dark sayings.
>
> The fear of the Lord is the beginning of knowledge, but fools despise wisdom and instruction.
>
> My son, hear the instruction of your father and forsake not the law of your mother.
>
> from Proverbs 1:1–9

CHAPTER 2

LEARNING ABOUT PRONOUNS

LESSON 2-A RECOGNITION OF PRONOUNS

• A *pronoun* is a word used as a substitute for a noun. Notice how awkward the sentence below sounds.

God gave God's Son to die for the sins of the world.

By using a pronoun the same sentence sounds much better.

God gave *His* Son to die for the sins of the world.

Pronouns are grouped in several different ways:

- personal pronouns
- demonstrative pronouns
- reflexive pronouns
- relative pronouns.
- indefinite pronouns
- interrogative pronouns
- intensive pronouns

EXERCISE 1

Write a definition of a pronoun in the space provided.

LESSON 2-B PERSONAL PRONOUNS

• *Personal pronouns* are those which indicate the speaker, the person spoken to, or the person or things spoken about. Personal pronouns may be identified by case, person, number and gender.

• CASES: There are three cases in the English language:
  nominative
  objective
  possessive

• PERSONS: There are three forms called persons:
  first person
  second person
  third person

• NUMBER: Personal pronouns have number:
  singular
  plural

• GENDER: There are three genders:
  masculine (male)
  feminine (female)
  neuter (inanimate)

EXERCISE 2

Study the charts below. Memorize all parts of the charts. Then answer the questions following the charts.

Nominative Case

(Used as subjects and predicate nominatives)*

	Singular	Plural
1st person	I	we
2nd person	you	you
3rd person	he, she, it	they

Possessive Case

(Used as adjectives)*

	Singular	Plural
1st person	my, mine	our, ours
2nd person	your, yours	your, yours
3rd person	his, her, hers, its	their, theirs

Objective Case

(Used as direct objects, indirect objects, and objects of prepositions)*

	Singular	Plural
1st person	me	us
2nd person	you	you
3rd person	him, her, it	them

EXERCISE 3

Write the nominative personal pronouns in the space provided.

EXERCISE 4

Write the possessive personal pronouns in the space provided.

EXERCISE 5

Write the objective personal pronouns in the space provided.

*These terms are discussed in detail in Part II, Chapters 9, 10, and 11.

EXERCISE 6

Fill in the blanks with the proper personal pronouns.

1. The first person, singular, nominative pronoun is ________.
2. The third person, plural, possessive pronoun is ________.
3. The first person, plural, nominative pronoun is ________.
4. The third person, masculine, singular, nominative pronoun is ________.
5. The third person, plural, objective pronoun is ________.
6. The second person, plural, objective pronoun is ________.
7. The first person, plural, possessive pronoun is ________.
8. The second person, plural, possessive pronoun is ________.
9. The third person, singular, feminine, objective pronoun is ________.
10. The first person, singular, possessive pronoun is ________.

EXERCISE 7

The three genders are ________, ________, and ________.

EXERCISE 8

Underline the personal pronouns in each of the following sentences.

1. And when they were come into the house, they saw the young child with Mary, his mother, and fell down, and worshipped him.
2. When they had opened their treasures, they presented unto him gifts: gold, frankincense, and myrrh.
3. And being warned of God in a dream that they should not return to Herod, they departed into their own country another way.
4. When they were departed, behold, the angel of the Lord appeared to Joseph in a dream saying, "Arise, and take the young child and his mother, and flee into Egypt, and stay there until I bring you word."
5. "For Herod will seek the young child to destroy him."
6. When he arose, he took the young child and his mother by night and departed into Egypt.
7. And they stayed there until the death of Herod that it might be fulfilled which was spoken of the Lord by the prophet saying, "Out of Egypt have I called my son."

from Matthew 2:11–15

LESSON 2-C INDEFINITE PRONOUNS

Indefinite pronouns are pronouns which do not relate to a person as clearly as personal pronouns do. Some indefinite pronouns are singular; some indefinite pronouns are plural; some indefinite pronouns are either singular or plural.

Examples:

a. Singular: another, anybody, anyone, anything, either, everybody, everyone, everything, much, neither, nobody, no one, nothing, one, other, somebody, someone, something, such.

b. Plural: both, few, many, several, others.

c. Either singular or plural: all, any, more, most, none, some.

EXERCISE 9

Underline all of the indefinite pronouns in the following sentences.

1. Because strait is the gate and narrow is the way which leadeth unto life, few there be that find it. (Matthew 7:14)
2. The wicked shall be turned into hell, and all the nations that forget God. (Psalms 9:17)
3. The Lord looked down from heaven upon the children of men to see if there were any that did understand and seek God. (Psalms 14:2)
4. They are all gone aside; they are all together become filthy; there is none that doeth good, no, not one. (Psalms 14:3)
5. You, Lord, have proved mine heart; you have visited me in the night; you have tried me, and shall find nothing; I am purposed that my mouth shall not transgress. (Psalms 17:3)
6. Some trust in chariots and some in horses; but we will remember the name of the Lord our God. (Psalms 20:7)
7. All they that be fat upon earth shall eat and worship; all shall bow before him; and none can keep alive his own soul. (Psalms 22:29)
8. Consider mine enemies; for they are many; and they hate me with cruel hatred. (Psalms 25:19)
9. For as many as are led by the Spirit of God, they are the sons of God. (Romans 8:14)
10. For there is nothing covered that shall not be revealed, neither hid that shall not be known. (Luke 12:2)

LESSON 2-D DEMONSTRATIVE PRONOUNS

The *demonstrative pronouns* are used to point out persons or things. There are four demonstrative pronouns: *this, that, these,* and *those.*

Sometimes *such* is used as a demonstrative pronoun.

This, that, these, those, and such can be used as *demonstrative adjectives* also. Notice the sentences below.

Examples:

a. And I (John) saw, and bare record that *this* is the Son of God. (*This* is a demonstrative pronoun.) John 1:34

b. And I (John) saw, and bare record that *this* man is the Son of God. (*This* is used as a demonstrative adjective.)

EXERCISE 10

Underline the demonstrative pronouns in the following sentences.

1. This is he that came by water and blood, even Jesus Christ. (John 5:6)
2. There are three that bear record in heaven, the Father, the Word, and the Holy Ghost; and these three are one. (I John 5:7)
3. And these write we unto you that your joy may be full. (I John 1:4)
4. That which we have seen and heard declare we unto you. (I John 1:3a)
5. Unto his disciples Jesus said, "Into whatsoever city you enter, and they receive you, eat such as are set before you." (Luke 10:8)
6. Sell that which you have and give alms; provide yourselves bags which wax not old. (Luke 12:33)
7. For all these have of their abundance cast in unto the offerings of God; but she of her penury has cast in all the living that she had. (Luke 21:4)
8. But Jesus called them unto him, and said, "Suffer little children to come unto me, and forbid them not; for of such is the kingdom of God. (Luke 18:16)
9. For the Son of man is come to seek and to save that which was lost. (Luke 19:10)

EXERCISE 11

Write the demonstrative pronouns in the space provided.

LESSON 2-E INTERROGATIVE PRONOUNS

The *interrogative pronouns* are pronouns used to ask questions. There are five interrogative pronouns: *who, whose, whom, which,* and *what.*

Sometimes students confuse the use of the words *whose* and *who's.* *Whose* is a possessive pronoun. *Who's* is a contraction for who is.

Examples:

a. Who's going to school?

b. Whose book is that?

Another problem arises with the use of *who* and *whom.* These two words are discussed later in the book. Refer to page 85.

EXERCISE 12

Write the interrogative pronouns in the space provided.

EXERCISE 13

Underline the interrogative pronouns in the following sentences.

1. Who has believed our report?
2. To whom is the arm of the Lord revealed? (Isaiah 53:1)
3. What is man that you are mindful of him? (Hebrews 2:6)
4. The Lord is my light and my salvation; whom shall I fear? Of whom shall I be afraid? (Psalm 27:1)
5. Who is this King of glory? The Lord of Hosts, he is the King of glory. (Psalm 24:10)
6. Which of you by taking thought can add one cubit unto your stature? (Matthew 6:27)
7. Which of the prophets was swallowed by a whale?
8. Whose rod was turned into a serpent?

LESSON 2-F INTENSIVE-REFLEXIVE PRONOUNS

The personal pronouns have another form called *intensive* and *reflexive* pronouns. The intensive pronouns intensify or emphasize the noun to which they refer. The reflexive pronouns return action to the subject.

The intensive-reflexive pronouns are as follows:

Singular	Plural
myself	ourselves
yourself	yourselves
himself, herself, itself	themselves

Examples:

a. I *myself* urged you to study. (intensive pronoun)

b. You did the work *yourself.* (reflexive pronoun)

c. The students *themselves* must do the work. (intensive pronoun)
d. The students will hurt *themselves* if they do not study. (reflexive pronoun)

EXERCISE 14

Write the intensive-reflexive pronouns in the space provided.

EXERCISE 15

Underline the intensive-reflexive pronouns in the following sentences.

1. For they themselves show of us what manner of entering in we had unto you and how you turned to God from idols to serve the living and true God. (I Thessalonians 1:9)
2. For yourselves, brethren, know our entrance in unto you, that it was not in vain. (I Thessalonians 2:1)
3. For Christ himself took our infirmities.
4. These ten times have you reproached me; you are not ashamed that you make yourselves strange to me. (Job 19:3)
5. Job said, "I abhor myself and repent in dust and ashes." (Job 42:1)
6. Therefore, the Lord himself shall give you a sign. (Isaiah 7:14a)
7. But we will give ourselves continually to prayer. (Acts 6:4a)

*NOTE: The intensive-reflexive pronouns are never used as subjects or compound direct objects in formal English.

Informal:	John and myself did it.
Formal:	John and I did it.
Informal:	He asked John and myself.
Formal:	He asked John and me.

LESSON 2-G RELATIVE PRONOUNS

Relative pronouns are those which relate to persons or objects. The most common relative pronouns are: *who, whose, whom, which,* and *that.* We shall study relative pronouns in detail in the chapter on complex sentences.

*These terms are discussed in detail in Part II, Chapters 9, 10, and 11.

Examples:

a. Matthew is the tax collector *who* wrote about the birth of Jesus.
b. Matthew is the publican *whose* name is also given as Levi.
c. The Jews are the people to *whom* the book of Matthew is addressed.
d. The key words *which* appear in Matthew are fulfilled, kingdom, and Kingdom of Heaven.
e. The apparent purpose of the book is to show *that* Jesus of Nazareth was the Kingly Messiah of Jewish prophecy.

EXERCISE 16

Write the relative pronouns in the space provided.

EXPLORING TRUTHS

Read Psalm 23. Look for the pronouns He (Thou) and me. Write all the things He (Thou) will do for His children. Write all the things we can expect from Him.

TEST ON PRONOUNS

Underline the pronouns in the following selection. Over the pronouns, write the kind of pronoun (personal, indefinite, demonstrative, interrogative, intensive-reflexive, relative) each one is.

1. Then Herod, when he saw that he was mocked of the wise men, was exceeding wroth, and sent forth, and slew all of the children that were in Bethlehem and in all of the coasts thereof, from two years old and under, according to the time which he had diligently enquired of the wise men.
2. Then was fulfilled that which was spoken by Jeremy, the prophet, saying,
3. In Rama was there a voice heard, lamentation, and weeping, and great mourning, Rachel weeping for her children, and would not be comforted, because they are not.
4. But when Herod was dead, behold, an angel of the Lord appeared in a dream to Joseph in Egypt,
5. Saying, "Arise, and take the young child and his mother, and go into the land of Israel: for they are dead which sought the young child's life."
6. And he arose, and took the young child and his mother and came into the land of Israel.
7. But when he heard that Archelaus did reign in Judaea in the room of his father Herod, he was afraid to go thither: not withstanding, being warned of God in a dream, he turned aside into the parts of Galilee.
8. And he came and dwelt in a city called Nazareth: that it might be fulfilled which was spoken by the prophets, 'He shall be called a Nazarene.'

from Matthew 2:16–23

CHAPTER 3

LEARNING ABOUT VERBS

LESSON 3-A RECOGNITION OF VERBS

- A *verb* is a word used that expresses action or shows a condition or state.

Verbs are classified in five different ways:

- action verbs
- linking verbs
- auxiliary verbs
- transitive verbs
- intransitive verbs

EXERCISE 1

In the space provided write a definition of a verb.

LESSON 3-B ACTION VERBS

Action verbs are words that show what action the subject is doing or what action is happening to the subject.

Examples:

a. The third chapter of "Matthew" *tells* about John the Baptist.

b. John *preached* about Jesus and repentence.

EXERCISE 2

Underline the action verbs in the following passage.

1. John the Baptist preached in the wilderness of Judaea.
2. Isaiah wrote about John the Baptist.
3. John prepared the way for the Lord Jesus.
4. John wore raiment of camel's hair and had a leather girdle about his loins.
5. He ate locust and wild honey.
6. Jerusalem and all Judaea went to meet John.
7. John baptized people in the Jordan River after they confessed their sins.
8. Many Pharisees and Sadducees came to John.
9. Who warned the Pharisees and Sadducees of the wrath to come?
10. John baptized with water unto repentance; but the one who comes after John will baptize with the Holy Ghost.

Matthew 3:1 (paraphrased)

LESSON 3-C LINKING VERBS

Linking verbs are important even though there are only a small number of them. Linking verbs relate one word to another. They link the noun or pronoun used as a subject of the sentence to the noun, pronoun, or adjective that follows the linking verb.

Examples:

a. Jesus *was* incarnate. (*Was* links Jesus and incarnate.)

b. Jesus *is* mighty. (*Is* links Jesus and mighty.)

c. Jesus *became* our Saviour. (*Became* links Jesus and Saviour.)

The verb *be* is the most commonly used linking verb. Memorize the following forms of the verb *be.*

- is
- am
- are
- was
- were
- shall be
- being
- will be
- have been
- has been
- had been
- shall have been
- will have been

Other verbs used as linking verbs are

- seem
- become
- appear
- remain
- get
- grow
- stay
- taste
- feel
- smell
- sound

EXERCISE 3

List fifteen verbs that could be used as linking verbs.

EXERCISE 4

Place a linking verb in each of the following sentences. Be certain that the words following the linking verbs mean the same thing as the noun or pronoun before the linking verbs.

1. The Bible __________ the Word of God.
2. Matthew __________ the author of the first book in the New Testament.
3. People __________ kind to one another.
4. Food __________ good for us when we __________ hungry.
5. Boys and girls __________ Christians when they receive Jesus as Saviour.

Sometimes linking verbs are used as action verbs. The way in which the verb is used in the sentence determines whether it is a linking verb or an action verb.

Examples:

a. The herb *tasted* bitter. (*Tasted* is a linking verb and *bitter* describes herb.)

b. The child *tasted* the herb. (*Tasted* is an action verb.)

EXERCISE 5

In the following sentences underline the *verbs* and write l.v. (linking verb) or a.v. (action verb) over the proper verbs.

Example:

l.v. a.v.
This *is* easy if you *studied* the list of verbs.

1. Noah felt afraid when he heard God's voice.
2. God spoke to Noah, and Noah became calm.
3. Noah built an ark.
4. All of Noah's family was safe in the ark.
5. Noah sounded a call for animals to come aboard.
6. The animals sounded happy in the ship.
7. God looked after the ark.
8. The dove looked for dry ground.
9. Noah removed the covering from the ark and looked for dry ground.
10. Noah and his family looked peaceful when the storm ended.

from Genesis 6:8–8:13

LESSON 3-D HELPING VERBS

A *helping verb* or an *auxiliary verb* is a verb that helps another verb. The word auxiliary means helping or aiding. The main verb plus the helping verb is called a *verb phrase*. Memorize the following helping verbs:

- am, is, are, was
- were, been, shall
- has, will, have
- should, had, might
- must, would, could
- may, do, does, did

Helping verbs help to show tense, voice, and mood.*

Examples:

a. The family *goes* to church. (*Goes* is the main verb.)

b. The children *are going* to church. (*Going* is the main verb; the helping verb is *are;* the verb phrase is *are going.*)

*(These terms are discussed in detail in Part II, Chapter 11.).

EXERCISE 6

Underline the verbs in the following sentences. Write l.v. (linking verb) or a. v. (action verb) over the proper verbs. Remember that some verbs consist of verb phrases. Be certain to include the verb phrases.

Example:

a.v. l.v.
John *declared* that Jesus *would be* mightier than he, and
a.v.
that Jesus *would burn* up the chaff with unquenchable fire.

1. Then Jesus came from Galilee to Jordan unto John for baptism.
2. When Jesus was baptized, he went up straightway out of the water; and, lo, the heavens were opened unto him, and he saw the Spirit of God descending like a dove, and the dove lighting upon him.
3. And, lo, a voice from heaven said, "This is my beloved Son in whom I am well pleased."
4. Then Jesus was led of the Spirit into the wilderness, and he was tempted of the devil.
5. After he fasted forty days, he was hungry.
6. The tempter came to him and said, "If you are the Son of God, command these stones to turn into bread."
7. Jesus replied, "Man shall not live by bread alone, but by every word that proceeds out of the mouth of God."
8. Satan tempted Jesus three times.
9. Jesus said, "It is written, 'You shall worship the Lord your God and him only shall you serve'."
10. Then the devil left Jesus and angels ministered unto him.

from Matthew 3:13–4:11

LESSON 3-E TRANSITIVE AND INTRANSITIVE VERBS

A *transitive verb* is a verb which has a receiver of its action.

Examples:

a. God *created* man and woman. (Man and woman receive the action of *created.*)
b. Man and woman *were created* by God. (Man and woman receive the action of *were created.*)

An *intransitive verb* has no receiver of action. All linking verbs are intransitive verbs. Action verbs which have no receiver of the action are intransitive verbs also.

Examples:

a. Adam and Eve *lived* in the Garden of Eden. (*Lived* is an action verb without a receiver of action.)
b. Adam and Eve *were* the first living human beings. (*Were* is a linking verb.)

EXERCISE 7

Underline the verbs in the following sentences and write tr. over the transitive verbs and write intr. over the intransitive verbs.

1. In the beginning God created the heaven and the earth.
2. At first, the earth was a shapeless, chaotic mass.
3. Darkness was upon the face of the deep.
4. The Spirit of God moved upon the face of the waters.
5. God said, "Let there be light, and there was light."
6. God was pleased with what he saw.
7. God divided the light from the darkness.
8. God called the light Day.
9. The darkness he called Night.
10. The evening and the morning were the first day.

from Genesis 1:1–5

EXPLORING TRUTHS

Read I, II, and III John. Look for the *linking verbs.* Write the word or words in front of the linking verb, the linking verb, and the word or words following the linking verb.

Example:

Verse	Words in Front of Linking Verb	Linking Verb	Words Following the Linking Verb
I John 1:4	joy	may be	full

What do these phrases mean to you personally?

TEST ON VERBS

1. Name at least ten verbs which may be used as linking verbs.

2. Name at least five verbs which may be used as helping verbs.

3. Underline the verbs and verb phrases in the following passage. Write tr. over the transitive verbs; write intr. over the intransitive verbs. Remember that linking verbs and action verbs which have no receiver of action are intransitive verbs.

   Example:

   A virtuous woman (intr.) *is* a crown to her husband; but she that (tr.) *makes* him ashamed (intr.) *is* as rottenness in his bones.

   a. A false balance is abomination to the Lord, but a just weight is his delight.

   b. When pride comes, then comes shame, but with the lowly is wisdom.

   c. The integrity of the upright shall guide them, but the perverseness of transgressors shall destroy them.

   d. Riches profit not in the day of wrath, but righteousness delivereth from death.

   e. The fruit of the righteous is a tree of life, and he that winneth souls is wise.

from Proverbs 11

CHAPTER 4

LEARNING ABOUT ADJECTIVES

LESSON 4-A RECOGNITION OF ADJECTIVES

• *An adjective* is a word used to describe or limit a noun or a pronoun.

There are two broad kinds of adjectives: adjectives that describe and adjectives that limit. The descriptive adjectives describe or tell what kind of noun or pronoun. The limiting adjectives tell how many, which one, or how much.

LESSON 4-B DESCRIPTIVE ADJECTIVES

A *descriptive adjective* modifies a noun or a pronoun. It may appear in the sentence before the noun it modifies, or it may appear after the noun it modifies.

Examples:

a. A *deceitful* and *wicked* heart needs to be cleansed.

b. The heart, *deceitful* and *wicked,* needs to be cleansed.

The descriptive adjective may also follow a linking verb.

Example:

The heart is *deceitful* and desperately *wicked.*

EXERCISE 1

Underline the descriptive adjectives in the following sentences.

1. The Garden of Eden was a beautiful place to live.
2. God made two great lights: the greater light to rule the day, and the lesser light to rule the night. (Genesis 1:16)
3. God made the waters bring forth moving creatures that had life, and fowl that flew above the earth in the open firmament of heaven. (Genesis 1:20)
4. God created large whales and every living thing that moves, after their kind, and every winged fowl, after his kind. (Genesis 1:21)
5. God made all sorts of wild animals.
6. Then God said, "Let us make man in our image." So God created man in his own image. (Genesis 1:26a, 27a)
7. God created male and female and gave them dominion over the whole earth.
8. God rested on the seventh day from all His work.
9. The Lord God planted a garden in Eden, and out of the ground the Lord God made to grow every tree that is pleasant to the sight and good for food. (Genesis 2:9)

10. And the Lord God said, "It is not good that the man should be alone; I will make him an help meet." (Genesis 2:18)

LESSON 4-C LIMITING ADJECTIVES

There are several forms of *limiting adjectives:* the articles, the demonstratives, the indefinites, the interrogatives, and the numerals.

The three words *a, an,* and *the* are called articles. They always precede a noun or a pronoun. *The* is called the definite article because it refers to one item; *a* and *an* are called indefinite articles because they do not limit the noun.

This, that, these, those, and *such* are called the demonstrative adjectives when they precede a noun. Refer to page 21 for a review of the difference between demonstrative adjectives and demonstrative pronouns.

The most common indefinite pronouns, *all, another, any, both, each, either, every, few, many, most, much, neither, no, other, several,* and *some,* can also be used as adjectives.

The indefinite adjectives usually precede the noun or pronoun which they modify.

The interrogative pronouns, *which, whose,* and *what,* may be used as limiting adjectives. Usually they precede the noun which they modify.

Numerals, words like *one, two, three,* or *first, second,* or *third,* are limiting adjectives when they precede a noun.

EXERCISE 2

The three articles are

1.
2.
3.

EXERCISE 3

Write the demonstrative adjectives in the space provided.

1.
2.
3.
4.
5.

EXERCISE 4

Underline the descriptive and limiting adjectives in the following sentences. Write P over the pronouns in the following sentences.

Example:

Out of the ground the Lord God formed every beast of the field, and every fowl of the air; and brought *them* unto Adam to see *what he* would call *them;* and *whatsoever* Adam called every *living* creature, *that* was the name thereof. (Genesis 2:19)

1. What did God create?
2. What garden did God create?
3. Who can understand His ways?
4. The Evolution Theory can not be proven.
5. That theory is contrary to Biblical teaching.
6. Those ideas developed by man are not pleasing to God.
7. All Scripture is given by inspiration of God and is profitable for doctrine, for reproof, for correction, for instruction in righteousness. (II Timothy 3:16)
8. All have sinned and come short of the glory of God. (Romans 3:23)
9. God looked down from heaven upon the children of men to see if there were any that did understand, that did seek God. (Psalms 53:2)
10. Everyone of them is gone back; they are altogether become filthy; there is none that doeth good, no, not one. (Psalms 53:3)

EXPLORING TRUTHS

Consider the adjectives which you have studied. Look in your Bible for other examples of adjectives like *all, some, good, evil.* Find verses containing noun phrases (a noun with adjectives) and apply them to your life.

Example:

All power is given unto me in heaven and in earth.
(Matthew 28:18)

Did Jesus really mean *ALL* power?

TEST ON ADJECTIVES

Underline the adjectives in the following sentences. Include the descriptive and limiting adjectives.

1. In Isaiah's vision, the Lord was sitting on a throne, high and lifted up.
2. Each of the seraphims above the throne had six wings.
3. They cried, "Holy, holy, holy is the Lord of hosts, the whole earth is full of his glory."
4. Isaiah exclaimed, "I am a man of unclean lips."
5. One seraphim, with a live coal in his hand, laid it on Isaiah's lips.
6. Then the seraphim said, "This has touched your lips, and your iniquity is taken away."
7. These sayings are true and the story is found in Isaiah 6.
8. Jesus said, "All power is given unto me in heaven and in earth."

from Matthew 28:18

CHAPTER 5

LEARNING ABOUT ADVERBS

LESSON 5-A RECOGNITION OF ADVERBS

• An *adverb* is a word which modifies a verb, adjective, or another adverb. Adverbs usually answer the following questions: where? how? when? why? to what extent? how much? *Not* is always an adverb.

Examples:

a. Where? — Let all bitterness and wrath and anger and clamour and evil speaking be put *away* from you. (Ephesians 4:31)

b. How? — See then, that you walk *circumspectly,* not as fools, but as wise. (Ephesians 5:15)

c. When? — *Now* is the accepted time; behold, *now* is the day of salvation. (II Corinthians 6:2)

d. To what extent? — Giving thanks *always* for all things unto God and the Father in the name of our Lord Jesus Christ. (Ephesians 5:20)

e. Negative. — Be *not* drunk with wine, wherein is excess, but be filled with the Spirit. (Ephesians 5:18)

EXERCISE 1

Underline the adverbs in the following sentences.

1. Grieve not the Holy Spirit of God. (Ephesians 4:30)
2. Henceforth, be no more children, tossed to and fro, and carried about with every wind of doctrine. (Ephesians 4:14)
3. Speaking the truth in love, you should grow up into him in all things. (Ephesians 4:15)
4. Christ is the head from whom the whole body fitly joined together makes increase of the body unto the edifying of itself in love. (Ephesians 4:16)
5. Hold fast the profession of your faith. (Hebrews 4:14c)
6. Run patiently the race which is set before you. (Hebrews 12:1b).
7. Christ gave himself freely for us.

8. Let us come boldly unto the throne of grace that we may obtain mercy and find grace to help in time of need. (Hebrews 4:16)

LESSON 5-B HOW ADVERBS ARE USED

1. Adverbs are words which modify verbs.

   Examples:

   a. We go to church *regularly.* (*Regularly* modifies the verb go.)
   b. *Thoughtfully* we sing praises to God. (*Thoughtfully* modifies sing.)
   c. We *never* sleep in church. (*Never* modifies sleep.)

2. Adverbs are words which modify adjectives.

   Examples:

   a. Children should be *very* careful to obey adults. (*Very* modifies the adjective careful.)
   b. Adults must be *especially* glad to help children. (*Especially* modifies glad.)
   c. That advice is not *too* difficult to follow. (*Too* modifies difficult.)

3. Adverbs are words which modify other adverbs.

   Examples:

   a. He quoted his verses *more* distinctly than I did. (*More* modifies distinctly.)
   b. To play the piano *very* skillfully demands hours of practice. (*Very* modifies skillfully.)

4. Sometimes a noun acts like an adverb. An adverbial noun is a noun which answers the questions when, where, how, or how much. The *adverbial noun,* however, uses the pattern of a regular noun to form a plural.

   Examples:

   a. Jesus walked many *miles* each day.
   b. I went out full, and the Lord hath brought me *home* again empty. (Ruth 1:21)

EXERCISE 2

Underline the adverbs and adverbial nouns in the following sentences.

1. Once an angel of God appeared to Manoah's wife.
2. Manoah, Samson's father, asked the man of God to come again unto him.

3. When the angel appeared, the wife of Manoah ran quickly to get her husband.
4. The angel told the wife that she would soon bare a child.
5. That child, Samson, would never drink strong drink, and he would not eat any unclean thing.
6. Samson grew to be quite strong.
7. Samson willfully disobeyed God and lost his power with God.
8. God is the same yesterday, today, and forever.
9. Watch for the adverb also in Scriptures.
10. The story of Samson is fully explained in the book of Judges in the Bible.

LESSON 5-C KINDS OF ADVERBS

In addition to the regular adverbs which we have just studied, there are three special types of adverbs: the *conjunctive adverb,* the *interrogative adverb,* and the *relative adverb.*

• *Conjunctive adverbs* are words which are used to connect two sentences. A semi-colon is used at the end of the first sentence; then, a comma follows the conjunctive adverb. The most common conjunctive adverbs are *accordingly, also, besides, consequently, furthermore, hence, however, indeed, likewise, moreover, nevertheless, still, then, thus,* and *therefore.* More details about conjunctive adverbs will be presented in the chapter on compound sentences. Page 151.

Examples:

a. Christ died for our sins; *therefore,* we ought to love Him with our whole body, soul, and spirit.
b. God loved us dearly; *consequently,* He sent His Son to die for our sins.

• *Interrogative adverbs* often modify verbs and they ask questions. They are easy to identify because there are only four common interrogative adverbs. They are *how, when, where,* and *why.*

Examples:

a. *How* can a person inherit eternal life?
b. *When* is a person old enough to receive Jesus Christ as Saviour?
c. *Where* may I find the key to happiness?
d. *Why* should Jesus love me?

• *Relative adverbs,* like relative pronouns, are few in number. The most commonly used relative adverbs are *when, where,* and *why.* We shall study relative adverbs in more detail in a later chapter. Page 155.

Examples:

a. Christmas is the time *when* we celebrate the birth of Jesus Christ.
b. Bethlehem is the place *where* Christ was born.
c. The reason *why* we celebrate His birth is because we love Him.

EXERCISE 3

Write five words which could be used as conjunctive adverbs in the space provided.

EXERCISE 4

Write four interrogative adverbs.

EXERCISE 5

Write three relative adverbs.

EXPLORING TRUTHS

As you read your Bible, look for adverbs. Ask God for a richer meaning of His Word through the extensive recognition of adverbs in the Scriptures. Be aware of words such as *also, then, too.* What new meaning do adverbs give to you as you read?

TEST ON ADVERBS

1. What five questions do adverbs answer?

   a.

   b.

   c.

   d.

   e.

2. What three parts of speech do adverbs modify?

   a.

   b.

   c.

3. Nouns which are used as adverbs are called __________ __________.

4. Underline the adverbs and adverbial nouns in the following passages.

   a. He which soweth sparingly shall reap also sparingly; and he which soweth bountifully shall reap also bountifully. (II Corinthians 9:6)

   b. Today if you will hear his voice, harden not your hearts, as in the provocation. (Hebrews 3:15)

   c. How shall we escape, if we neglect so great salvation? (Hebrews 2:3a)

   d. Oh, that I had wings like a dove! Then would I fly away and be at rest. (Psalms 55:6)

   e. Evening, morning, and at noon will I pray and cry aloud; and he shall hear my voice. (Psalms 55:17)

   f. Awake up, my glory; awake psaltery and harp; I myself will awake early. (Psalms 57:8)

   g. God only is my rock and my salvation; he is my defense; I shall not be moved. (Psalms 62:6)

   h. All that will live godly in Christ Jesus shall suffer persecution. (II Timothy 3:13)

   i. This I say then, "Walk in the Spirit, and you shall not fulfill the lust of the flesh." (Galatians 5:16)

   j. Stand fast therefore in the liberty wherewith Christ has made us free and be not entangled again with the yoke of bondage. (Galatians 5:1)

CHAPTER 6

LEARNING ABOUT PREPOSITIONS

LESSON 6-A RECOGNITION OF PREPOSITIONS

• A *preposition* is a word used to show a relation between a noun or pronoun and some other word in a sentence.

Examples:

a. *In* the beginning God created the heaven and the earth.

b. The earth was *without* form.

c. Darkness was *upon* the face *of* the deep.

Notice that the preposition is never used alone. It must be accompanied by a noun or a pronoun called the *object of the preposition.* When the object is missing, the preposition becomes an *adverb.*

Examples:

a. The dove flew *over.* (Adverb telling where)

b. The dove flew *over* his head. (preposition)

There are many prepositions in the English language. Listed below are some of the common prepositions.

about	around	down	like	toward
above	at	during	of	under
across	beside	except	off	up
after	between	for	on	upon
against	beyond	from	over	with
along	but (except)	in	through	within
among	by	into	to	without

Sometimes prepositions consist of more than one word.

Examples:

according to, in spite of, instead of, on account of

LESSON 6-B RECOGNITION OF PREPOSITIONAL PHRASES

• A *phrase* is a group of words. When the group of words is made up of a *preposition,* a *noun* or *pronoun,* and sometimes *adjectives* placed between the preposition and the noun or pronoun, a *prepositional phrase* exists.

Examples:

a. *In the beginning* God created the heaven and the earth. (*In* is the preposition, *the* is an adjective, and *beginning* is the object of the preposition.)

b. The earth was *without form.* (*Without* is the preposition, and *form* is the object of the preposition.)

EXERCISE 1

Underline the prepositional phrases in the following sentences and put a P over the prepositions.

Example:

If *in this life* only we have hope *in Christ,* we are *of all men* most miserable. (I Corinthians 15:19)

1. The Spirit of God moved upon the face of the waters.
2. God divided the light from the darkness.
3. God put the firmament in the midst of the waters and let the firmament divide the waters from the waters.
4. God made the firmament and divided the waters which were under the firmament from the waters which were above the firmament.
5. God called the dry land Earth, and the gathering together of the waters called He Seas.
6. God let the fruit tree yield fruit after his own kind, whose seed is in itself, upon the earth.

from Genesis 1

7. Do you believe that I am in the Father, and the Father in me?
8. The words that I speak unto you, I speak not of myself, but the Father that dwells in me, he does the work.
9. Believe me for the very work's sake.
10. Verily, verily, I say unto you, he that believes on me, the works that I do shall he do also; and greater works than these shall he do because I go unto my Father.

from John 14:10-13

EXPLORING TRUTHS

Prepositions are important little words. Consider the difference between *of* and *with* in the following sentences.

1. Have you made peace *with* God?
2. Do you know the peace *of* God?

Also, think about the use of the word *in* in the book of John.

TEST ON PREPOSITIONS

I. Name at least 15 words which can be used as prepositions.

a. i.
b. j.
c. k.
d. l.
e. m.
f. n.
g. o.
h.

II. A prepositional phrase is a group of words made up of a ________, a ________ or ________, and sometimes an ________ to modify the object of the preposition.

III. Underline the prepositional phrases in the following sentences.

a. And we know that all things work together for good to them that love God, to them who are the called according to *his* purpose. (Romans 8:28)

b. But as many as received him, to them gave he power to become the sons of God, *even* to them that believe on his name: (John 1:12)

c. Neither is there salvation in any other: for there is none other name under heaven given among men, whereby we must be saved. (Acts 4:12)

d. Thou wilt keep *him* in perfect peace, *whose* mind *is* stayed *on thee:* because he trusteth in thee. (Isaiah 26:3)

e. Behold, I stand at the door, and knock: if any man hear my voice, and open the door, I will come in to him, and will sup with him, and he with me. (Revelation 3:20)

CHAPTER 7

LEARNING ABOUT CONJUNCTIONS

LESSON 7-A RECOGNITION OF CONJUNCTIONS

• A *conjunction* is a word used to connect words, phrases, and clauses. There are three different kinds of conjunctions.

The three kinds of conjunctions are *coordinating conjunctions, correlative conjunctions,* and *subordinating conjunctions.*

LESSON 7-B COORDINATING CONJUNCTIONS

• *Coordinating conjunctions* — Seven words are used as coordinating conjunctions:

- and
- but
- or
- nor
- for
- so
- yet

They are called coordinating conjunctions because they connect words or phrases or clauses that are of the same grammatical type.

Examples:

a. Ananias *and* Sapphira were husband *and* wife. (*And* connects two nouns.)

b. Were they clever *or* foolish? (*Or* connects two adjectives.)

c. They sold their possessions; *yet* they kept a portion for themselves. (*Yet* connects two main clauses or sentences.)

EXERCISE 1

Name the seven coordinating conjunctions.

EXERCISE 2

Underline the coordinating conjunctions in the following sentences.

1. Satan had filled Ananias's heart and told him to keep back part of the price of the land.
2. Peter said to Ananias, "Thou hast not lied unto men but unto God."
3. Did Ananias sin against man or against God?
4. Ananias was stricken dead, for he had sinned grievously and great fear came upon everyone who heard these things.
5. Sapphira also lied to Peter, and she, too, fell dead.

6. They did not fool men, nor did they fool God.
7. Following this, many signs and wonders were done by the apostles.

from Acts 5

LESSON 7-C CORRELATIVE CONJUNCTIONS

● *Correlative conjunctions* — Conjunctions which are used in pairs to connect related words are called correlatives or correlative conjunctions. The most common examples are the following:

- either............... or
- neither .... nor
- not only....... but also
- both............... and

Example:

Neither Ananias *nor* his wife Sapphira thought their sin would be discovered.

EXERCISE 3

Write the correlative conjunctions in the space provided.

EXERCISE 4

Underline the pairs of correlative conjuctions in the following sentences.

1. Peter told Sapphira that not only had Ananias been smitten of God, but that she also would be smitten.
2. Both Ananias and Sapphira were disobedient.
3. God requires not only faith but also complete surrender if we want His fullest joy.

LESSON 7-D SUBORDINATING CONJUNCTIONS

● *Subordinating conjunctions* — Subordinating conjunctions are introductory words used in complex and compound-complex sentences. They are dealt with in another advanced grammar section. Subordinating conjunctions are mentioned here only to alert the student to their existence. 154

Examples:

a. *If* you live after the flesh, you shall die.
b. To be spiritually minded is life and peace *because* the carnal mind is enmity against God. (Romans 8:7)

EXPLORING TRUTHS

Notice which Old Testament books begin with a conjunction. What hint does the use of conjunctions give you about the place of the book in the Bible?

TEST ON CONJUNCTIONS

Underline the conjunctions in the following passages.

1. I will extol thee, O Lord, for thou has lifted me up.
(Psalm 30:1)
2. Be of good courage and he shall strengthen your heart.
(Psalm 31:24)
3. I sought in mine heart to give myself unto wine, yet acquainting my heart with wisdom.
4. I made me great works and builded me houses.
5. But I looked on all the works that my hands had wrought, and behold, all was vanity. (Ecclesiastes 2:3, 4, 11)
6. Both wisdom and money are defenses, but wisdom gives life.
(Ecclesiastes 7:12)
7. Fear God and keep his commandments, for this is the whole duty of man. (Ecclesiastes 12:13)

CHAPTER 8

LEARNING ABOUT INTERJECTIONS

LESSON 8-A RECOGNITION OF INTERJECTIONS

• An *interjection* is a word that expresses emotion and that has no grammatical relation with the rest of the sentence.

Examples:

a. *Oh,* I see.

b. *Well!* Do it.

Interjections are punctuated with a comma or an exclamation mark depending on the emotion expressed.

EXERCISE 1

Underline the interjections in the following sentences.

1. Behold, I stand at the door and knock. (Revelation 3:20a)
2. Alas! I am unclean.
3. But, oh, that I might know Him who to know is life eternal.
4. At last I have found Him. Hurrah!

LESSON 8-B LEARNING ABOUT PARENTHETICAL EXPRESSIONS

• A *parenthetical expression* is a word or group of words which interrupts a sentence and has no grammatical relation to the rest of the sentence. The following words are examples of parenthetical expressions:

also	likewise
at least	nevertheless
as I was saying	of course
for example	on the other hand
for instance	on the whole
however	perhaps
indeed	therefore
in fact	too
in my opinion	to tell the truth
I suppose	

• *Parenthetical expressions* are usually separated from the rest of the sentence by commas. Commas are not used in parenthetical expressions that do not require a pause in reading.

Examples:

a. *But this I say,* he which soweth sparingly shall reap *also* sparingly. (II Corinthians 9:6)
b. Be ye *therefore* followers of God, as dear children. (Ephesians 5:1)

EXERCISE 2

Name at least 5 expressions that can be used as parentheticals.

1.
2.
3.
4.
5.

EXERCISE 3

Underline the parenthetical expressions in the following sentences.

1. Stand therefore, having you loins girt about with truth. (Ephesians 6:14)
2. Some indeed preach Christ even of envy and strife. (Philippians 1:15)
3. And I intreat thee also, true yokefellow, help those women which labored with me in the Gospel. (Philippians 4:3)
4. And this I say, lest any man should beguile you with enticing words. (Colossians 2:4)
5. Likewise, you younger, submit yourselves unto the elder. (I Peter 5:5a)

EXPLORING TRUTHS

Look for the interjection *behold* in The Revelation. How many times does it appear? Why do you suppose it is used so frequently?

TEST ON INTERJECTIONS

Read the following verses from the *Bible*. In the space on the right, write the interjection found in each verse.

1. Job 4:3 ______________
2. Job 6:8 ______________
3. Job 13:1 ______________
4. Job 15:4 ______________
5. Job 16:21 ______________
6. Job 18:5 ______________
7. Job 21:27 ______________
8. Job 23:3 ______________
9. Job 25:14 ______________
10. Job 32:12 ______________
11. Job 33:29 ______________
12. Job 34:12 ______________
13. Job 36:5 ______________

FINAL TEST ON PART I

I. Name the eight parts of speech in the English language.

1.
2.
3.
4.
5.
6.
7.
8.

II. Match the following columns.

a. Adjective	1. Names a person, place, thing, or idea.	________
b. Preposition	2. Shows a relation between two words.	________
c. Interjection	3. Shows action and is needed to make a sentence.	________
d. Adverb	4. Answers the questions how, when, or where.	________
e. Noun	5. Connects two nouns or pronouns.	________
f. Verb	6. Describes a noun or a pronoun.	________
g. Pronoun	7. Takes the place of a noun.	________
h. Conjunction	8. Shows strong feeling.	________

III. Name the three articles.

1.
2.
3.

IV. Tell whether the underlined nouns in the following sentences are proper or common. Write PR over each proper noun and CM over each common noun.

Jesus grew up in (1) *Nazareth* with his (2) *mother* and (3) *father.* His father was a (4) *carpenter.* (5) *Mary* was a gentle (6) *woman.* (7) *Jesus* had several (8) *brothers.* Probably (9) *James* was one of his brothers.

V. Name the three cases in the English language.

1.
2.
3.

VI. The three genders in the English language are

1.
2.
3.

VII. The four demonstrative adjectives are

1.
2.
3.
4.

VIII. Name at least five indefinite pronouns.

1.
2.
3.
4.
5.

IX. List ten verbs that could be used as linking verbs.

1.
2.
3.
4.
5.
6.
7.
8.
9.
10.

X. The seven coordinating conjunctions are

1.
2.
3.
4.
5.
6.
7.

XI. In the space at the right, write the part of speech of the underlined word. Each sentence has two or more answers.

1. Jesus is the *light of* the world. __________ __________
2. Men do *not light* a candle and put it under a bushel __________ __________
3. Even a *light* burden *can be* heavy. __________ __________
4. Take *your burden* to the Lord. __________ __________
5. Do not *burden* yourself *with* worry. __________ __________
6. *The* Lord will be your *burden* carrier. __________ __________
7. Can *you* believe *these* truths? __________ __________
8. *These* are *only* some of the good __________ __________
   things in the *Bible.* __________ __________
9. *Alas, it* is good for me to study. __________ __________
10. Studying grammar *is* easy and *helpful.* __________ __________

PART II

USING PARTS OF SPEECH

In Part I, Chapters 1-8, the eight basic parts of speech were discussed. Now it is important to understand how each part of speech is used to develop a sentence.

CHAPTER 9

MORE LEARNING ABOUT NOUNS

Nouns can be used in many ways and can be found anywhere in a sentence. Consider the use of the name Jesus in the following sentences:

1. *Jesus* is the Son of God. (Subject of the verb *is*)
2. The Son of God is *Jesus.* (Predicate nominative)
3. Joseph and Mary took *Jesus* to Egypt. (Direct object of the verb *took*)
4. Have you given *Jesus* your heart? (Indirect object of the verb *have given*)
5. Have you given your heart to *Jesus?* (Object of the preposition *to*)
6. *Jesus'* mother was Mary. (Possessive)
7. The Son of God, *Jesus,* came to earth to redeem mankind. (Appositive)
8. *Jesus,* I thank you for dying for me. (Noun of direct address)

Now concentrate on each of the above uses of nouns. In the English language, the nouns do not change their forms, except in the possessive case. However, pronouns do change forms; therefore, all that is learned about noun usage will be very important in the study of pronouns.

LESSON 9-A USING NOUNS AS SUBJECTS

● A *subject* of a sentence is a word or group of words which names the person, place, thing, or idea about which something is said. The subject usually precedes the verb, but sometimes, as in an inverted sentence or in an interrogative sentence, the subject appears in other places in the sentence.

Examples:

(Subject)
a. *Jesus* chose Peter and Andrew to be fishers of men. (Normal word order)

(Subject)
b. Did *Jesus* choose Peter and Andrew as workers? (Interrogative sentence)

(Subject)
c. Down by the Sea of Galilee walked *Jesus.* (Inverted word order)

Sometimes the subject of a sentence consists of two or more words connected by *and* or *or.* These connected subjects are known as *compound subjects.*

Example:

Peter and *Andrew* followed Jesus. (Peter and Andrew are the subjects of the verb *followed.*)

EXERCISE 1

Underline the subjects in the following sentences. Be certain to check your answers by asking, "Who is doing the action? Or, about whom or what is the sentence talking?"

1. Later Jesus saw two other fishermen.
2. James and John were their names.
3. These men were the sons of Zebedee.
4. The fame of Jesus went throughout all Syria.
5. Many sick people came to Jesus for healing.
6. Travelling all around Galilee, Jesus healed the sick.
7. A great multitude of people followed Jesus from the surrounding country.

Story from Matthew 4:18-25

EXERCISE 2

Now underline the subjects in the following interrogative sentences.

1. Did Jesus see two fishermen?
2. Were James and John the sons of Zebedee?
3. Was Jesus able to heal the sick?
4. Have you read this story in Matthew 4?
5. Are you willing to follow Jesus?

- Sometimes the words *there* and *here* introduce English sentences. They are called *expletives* and are never used as the subject of a sentence.

EXERCISE 3

Underline the subjects in the following sentences.

1. There were many sick people who followed Jesus for healing.
2. Here is an exciting example of the grace and mercy of Jesus.
3. There is a river, the streams whereof shall make glad the city of God. (Psalms 46:4a)
4. There is no peace, saith my God, to the wicked. (Psalms 57:21)
5. There shall come forth a rod out of the stem of Jesse, and a Branch shall grow out of his roots. (Isaiah 11:1)

EXERCISE 4

Underline the subjects in the following sentences.

1. Paul wrote a letter to Philemon.
2. There were other Christians worshiping with Philemon.

3. Apphia and Archippus belonged to the household of faith.
4. Do Paul's letters begin with a salutation?
5. There was a spiritual relationship between Paul and Onesimus.
6. Onesimus was a servant, and he had been unfaithful to his master.
7. Paul urged Philemon to forgive Onesimus.
8. Were Onesimus, Philemon, and Paul of equal value to God?
9. God loves all men, but God hates sin.
10. Obedience, sympathy, and brotherhood should obliterate class distinctions.

from the book of Philemon

LESSON 9-B USING NOUNS AS PREDICATE NOMINATIVES

• A *predicate nominative* is a noun, pronoun, or adjective that completes the meaning of a linking verb. Refer to page 28 if you need to review the linking verbs. The predicate nominative always explains or describes the subject. Some books use the term *subject complement* or *subjective complement* rather than predicate nominative.

Examples:

(Subject)
a. James and John were *brothers.* (*Brothers* is the predicate nominative because it means the same thing as *James* and *John* and follows the linking verb *were.*)

(Subject)
b. They became *followers* of Jesus. (*Followers* is the predicate nominative because it explains *they* and follows the linking verb *became.*)

EXERCISE 5

Write as many linking verbs as you can.

EXERCISE 6

Underline the *subjects* in the following sentences and write P.N. over the *predicate nominatives* (subject complements). Remember that a predicate nominative is a noun, pronoun, or adjective that follows a linking verb and means the same as the subject or describes the subject. The first one has been done for you.

P.N.
1. For the preaching of the cross is to them that perish *foolishness.*
2. But unto us who are saved it is the power of God.
(I Corinthians 1:18)
3. Jesus Christ is the same yesterday, today, and forever.
4. Faith is the substance of things hoped for.
5. The angels are ministering spirits, sent forth to minister for them who shall be heirs of salvation. (Hebrews 1:14)
6. Jesus Christ, in whom there was no sin, became sin for us.
7. For to me to live is Christ, and to die is gain.
(Philippians 1:21)
8. This is the day which the Lord has made.
9. Jesus Christ is the vine; we are the branches.
10. A redeemed person becomes the apple of God's eye.

NOTE: The form of the noun used as a predicate nominative doesn't change. However, pronouns do change their forms with their usage;

therefore, it is important to recognize predicate nominatives in order to speak formal English correctly.

LESSON 9-C USING NOUNS AS DIRECT OBJECTS

- The *direct object* of the verb is a noun or pronoun that receives the action of the verb and answers the questions *What* or *Whom.*

Examples:

(Direct Object)

a. Men should praise the *Lord.* (*Lord* receives the action of praise and answers the question *Whom.*)

(Direct Object)

b. The Lord takes *pleasure* in them that fear him. (*Pleasure* receives the action of the verb takes and answers the question *What.*)

EXERCISE 7

Underline the *subject* once in the following sentences and write D. O. above the *direct object.* Remember that the direct object always follows an action verb and receives the action of that verb. Usually the direct object follows the verb, but in an inverted sentence or in an interrogative sentence, the direct object may precede the verb. The first example has been completed for you.

D.O.

1. No person should take the *name* of the Lord in vain.
2. You shall have no other gods before me.
3. You shall not make unto yourself any graven image.
4. You shall not bow down yourself to idols or serve them.
5. The Lord will show mercy unto thousands of them that love him and keep his commandments.
6. You shall remember the sabbath day to keep it holy.
7. Everyone should honor his father and mother.
8. The fifth commandment has a promise.
9. We should not kill; we should not commit adultery; we should not steal; we should not bear false witness against our neighbours.
10. No Christian should covet his neighbour's house nor his neighbour's wife, nor his manservant, nor his maidservant, nor any thing that is his neighbour's.

based on the Ten Commandments, Exodus 20

EXERCISE 8'

Underline the *subject* once, write *P.N.* over the words used as *predicate nominatives* and write D.O. over the *direct objects* in the following sentences.

Example:

Christians are the *salt* (P.N.) of the earth, but if the *salt* has lost its *savour* (D.O.), *it* is *good* (P.N) for nothing.

1. When Christ saw the multitudes following him, he opened his mouth and taught the people.
2. Blessed are the poor in spirit; for theirs is the kingdom of heaven.
3. Blessed are the meek; for they shall inherit the earth.
4. Blessed are the merciful; for they shall obtain mercy.
5. Christians are the light of the world.
6. Men do not light a candle and put the candle under a bed.
7. Rather, they put the candle on a candlestick, and it gives light.
8. Christians should let their light shine before men.
9. Then all people will see a Christian's good work.
10. Good works glorify our Father who is in heaven.

based on the Beatitudes in Matthew 5

LESSON 9-D USING NOUNS AS INDIRECT OBJECTS

• The *indirect object* of the verb is used after certain verbs, such as give, write, bring, and find. The *indirect object* is a noun or pronoun that tells *to whom* or *for whom* something is done.

Do not confuse the indirect object with a prepositional phrase. The indirect object always precedes the direct object. When either of the two words, *to* or *for*, is added to the sentence, the word order is changed and a prepositional phrase is made.

Examples:

a. I give *God* the glory for my salvation. (The indirect object is *God* because *God* tells *to whom* I give glory.)
b. I give the glory for my salvation *to God.* (*God* has become the object of the preposition *to.*)
c. Paul wrote *Timothy* a letter. (*To whom* did Paul write? To *Timothy,* the indirect object.)
d. Paul wrote a letter *to Timothy.* (The word *to* is mentioned and *Timothy* becomes the object of the preposition *to.*)

EXERCISE 9

Underline the *subject* once, write D.O. above the *direct object,* and write I.O. above the *indirect object.* The first one has been done for you.

I.O. D.O.
1. *Paul* wrote *Timothy* a *letter.*
2. Everyone should give God a tithe of his salary.
3. God supplied Bezaleel wisdom to build the tabernacle.
4. God told Moses the dimensions for the building.
5. The Israelites brought their leaders an excessive amount of offerings.
6. The children of Israel showed the finished tabernacle and equipment to Moses.
7. The writer of Exodus tells us the story of the tabernacle.
8. The Lord also spoke many commandments to Moses.
9. Then God gave Moses two tables of testimony.

from Exodus 35

LESSON 9-E USING NOUNS AS OBJECTS OF PREPOSITIONS

• The *object of the preposition* is the noun or pronoun that follows a preposition. Refer to page 47 if you have forgotten what a preposition is. A *prepositional phrase* is the group of words consisting of a preposition, modifier, and the object of the preposition.

Example:

(prep.) (mod.) (O.P.) (prep.) (O.P.)
If a person looks *(on a woman)* to lust *(after her),* he has committed adultery.

EXERCISE 10

In the space below write at least 10 words which can be used as prepositions. Check your answers with the prepositions listed on page 47.

EXERCISE 11

Place parentheses around the prepositional phrases in the following sentences, and write O.P. above the object of the preposition.

Example:

(O.P.)
If your right eye offends you, pluck it out and cast it (from *you.)*

NOTE: When the preposition has no object, that preposition becomes an adverb. See page 47. The word *out* in the above example is an adverb.

1. For it is profitable for you that one of your members should perish, and not that your whole body should be cast into hell.

2. It has been said, "An eye for an eye, and a tooth for a tooth."
3. But Jesus said, "You should not resist evil, but whoever shall smite you on the right cheek, turn to him the other also."
4. Love your enemies, bless them that curse you, and do good to them that hate you.
5. Then you will be the children of your Father who is in heaven.
6. Take heed that you do not do your alms before men.
7. Rather, do your alms in secret.

from Matthew 5 and 6

EXERCISE 12

Now try to analyze the following sentences by selecting the subject, the indirect object, the direct object, the object of the preposition, and the predicate nominative. Underline the subject once, write I.O. above the indirect object, write D.O. above the direct object, write O.P. above the object of the preposition, and P.N. above the predicate nominative.

Example:

When you pray, shut the (D.O.) *door* and enter into your (O.P.) *closet* and pray to your (O.P.) *Father* in (O.P.) *secret,* for God is a (P.N.) *rewarder* of (O.P.) *those* who trust (D.O.) *him.*

1. Our Father is in heaven.
2. Hallowed is his name.
3. His will should be done in earth, as it is in heaven.
4. He gives us our daily bread.
5. He forgives us our debts, as we forgive our debtors.
6. He leads us not into temptation, but delivers us from evil.
7. To God belong the kingdom, the power, and the glory forever.
8. Do not be a hypocrite when you fast.
9. Hypocrites disfigure their faces so that men may see what they are doing.
10. Christians should fast in secret.
11. God will reward them openly.
12. Our God is a searcher of hearts.

from Matthew 6

LESSON 9-F USING NOUNS AS POSSESSIVES

• A *possessive noun* shows ownership. There are at least 8 rules for forming the possessive case of nouns.

Learn the following rules for forming possessives.

a. To form the possessive of any singular noun, add an apostrophe and *s* to the noun.

Singular nouns	Possessive Case
disciple	disciple's robe
master	master's choice
James	James's book

NOTE: Some authorities state that only an apostrophe is necessary to make a proper name ending in *-s* into a possessive. Thus, James's or James' would be correct. However, it is always safe to use *rule a* as given above.

b. To form the possessive of a plural noun which ends in *s*, add an apostrophe only.

Plural nouns	Possessive Case
girls	girls' coats
students	students' projects
choirs	choirs' booklets

c. To form the possessive of a plural noun which does not end in *s*, add an apostrophe and s.

Plural nouns	Possessive Case
men	men's desires
women	women's clothing
sheep	sheep's wool

d. To form the possessive for two or more nouns in a series, the last name only is made possessive. However, if the ownership is separate, both names must be made possessive.

Mary and Martha's house (jointly owned) — Mary's and Martha's houses (each owns a house)

e. To form the possessive of a compound or hyphenated noun, put the apostrophe and *s* after the last word.

mother-in-law's car — Lord of Lord's jewels

f. To form the possessive of a non-living thing, use a phrase with the word *of*.

the top *of* the box (not box's top)

g. To form the possessive of nouns of measurement, follow the regular rules.

one week's notice — two weeks' notice

h. An apostrophe (') or an apostrophe s ('s) does not need to be used in the name of an institution, organization, or geographic location unless it is a part of the official title.

teachers organization	United States Armed Forces
Pikes Peak	Young Men's Christian Association

NOTE: Never use an apostrophe with the possessive pronouns.

This coat is *yours.* (Not your's)

EXERCISE 13

Supply the possessive form wherever it is needed in the following examples. If no possessive is needed, do not mark the phrase.

1. Adam and Eves home ____________________
2. Gods blessings ____________________
3. Noahs ark ____________________
4. wages of sin ____________________
5. a moments pleasure ____________________
6. This is theirs ____________________
7. father-in-laws car ____________________
8. a Christian attitude ____________________
9. fishermens boats ____________________
10. its value ____________________

LESSON 9-G USING NOUNS AS APPOSITIVES

- An *appositive* is a noun or noun phrase which follows a word and denotes (identifies, explains, or describes) the same person, place, or thing. An *appositional phrase* is always set off by commas; a single appositive doesn't always need a comma.

Examples:

a. The writer of Genesis, *Moses,* gives us the story of creation. (*Moses* is the appositive.)

b. Moses, *the writer of Genesis,* gives us the story of creation. (The phrase in apposition is *the writer of Genesis.*)

c. The writer *Moses* does not give a detailed account of creation. (No need for a comma around the appositive *Moses.*)

EXERCISE 14

Punctuate the following sentences which contain appositives and underline the noun in apposition. The first one has been done for you.

1. Have you read Genesis, the <u>book</u> of beginnings?
2. The first man and woman Adam and Eve are described in Genesis.
3. The character of the Tempter Satan is also described.
4. God's plan of salvation the promise of a coming Redeemer is explained.
5. Genesis relates the events of the Flood a destructive force which God permitted.

6. The book also records God's mercy the rainbow covenant.
7. At Babel the site of a tall tower God allowed a confusion of tongues and scattered the people.
8. Abraham a friend of God left his home at God's command.
9. Abraham the Father of the Faithful was blessed by God.
10. Do you know the story of Enoch the man who walked with God?
11. Two other characters in the book of Genesis Jacob and Joseph were transformed by God's grace.

EXERCISE 15

The use of appositives marks a mature speaker or writer. The appositive combines two simple thoughts into one sentence.

Try combining the following set of sentences into one sentence. Sometimes you will have to add additional words. The first one has been done for you.

1. Adam and Eve were the first man and woman. They lived in the Garden of Eden.

Answer:

Adam and Eve, the first man and woman, lived in the Garden of Eden.

2. Noah was the ark builder. He was ridiculed by his contemporaries.

Answer:

3. Cain brought an offering of the fruit of the ground to the Lord. The Lord had no respect unto his offering.

Answer:

4. The Lord respected Abel's offering. Abel brought of the firstlings of his flock and the fat thereof.

Answer:

5. Methuselah lived nine hundred sixty and nine years. He was Enoch's son.

Answer:

6. Everyone should memorize Genesis 3:15. Genesis 3:15 is the first Messianic Prophecy.

Answer:

7. According to the Bible, capital punishment should be allowed. Genesis 9:6 supplies the Christian with evidence.

Answer:

8. Jacob was a crafty young man. He secured his birthright by duping Esau.

Answer:

9. Later Jacob became a man of prayer. His life was transformed.

Answer:

10. Joseph was Jacob's son. He became a renowned ruler in Egypt.

Answer:

11. Abraham trusted God completely. He left his home in Ur to follow God.

Answer:

LESSON 9-H USING NOUNS AS NOUNS OF DIRECT ADDRESS

• A *noun of direct address* is the noun which indicates the person addressed. It is always separated from the rest of the sentence by a comma.

Example:

Father, we thank you for your goodness to us. (*Father* is the person addressed.)

EXERCISE 16:

Punctuate and underline the nouns of direct address in the following sentences.

1. Not everyone that says unto me, "Lord Lord shall enter the kingdom of heaven, but he that does the will of my Father."
from Matthew 7:21
2. The centurion said, "Jesus my servant is sick at home. Please come and heal him."
3. Jesus answered, Sir I have not found so great faith in all of Israel."
from Matthew 8:5-10
4. A certain scribe said, "Master I will follow you."
5. His disciples came to Jesus in the midst of a storm at sea and said, "Lord save us; we perish."
6. Jesus answered, "Why are you fearful you of little faith?"
from Matthew 8:23-27

EXERCISE 17

Now try to analyze the following sentences by telling how each underlined noun is used. In the space on the right indicate whether the nouns are used as subject, predicate nominative, direct object, indirect object, object of preposition, appositive, possessive, or noun of direct address. Use abbreviations if you wish. The first one has been done for you.

1. (a) *Jesus* entered into a (b) *ship* and came into his own (c) *country.*
   a. Subject
   b. Obj. of prep.
   c. Obj. of prep.

2. (d) *Jesus* knew their (e) *thoughts.*
   d. ________
   e. ________

3. Why do you think (f) *evil* in your (g) *hearts?*
   f. ________
   g. ________

4. The (h) *Son of Man,* (i) *Jesus Christ,* has (j) *power* on (k) *earth* to forgive (l) *sins.*
   h. ________
   i. ________
   j. ________
   k. ________
   l. ________

5. (m) *Jesus* healed the sick (n) *man.*
   m. ________
   n. ________

6. The (o) *multitude's* (p) *reaction* was a (q) *testimony* which glorified (r) *God.*
   o. ________
   p. ________
   q. ________
   r. ________

7. (s) *Lord,* give this (t) *believer* a clean (u) *heart.*
   s. ________
   t. ________
   u. ________

LESSON 9-I USING NOUNS AS OBJECTIVE COMPLEMENTS

- The *objective complement* is a noun or adjective that completes the meaning of the direct object. The objective complement follows such verbs as *appoint, call, choose, find, make, name,* and *think.*

Example:

Mary named the *baby Jesus.* (*Baby* is the direct object and *Jesus* is the objective complement.)

LESSON 9-J USING NOUNS AS RETAINED OBJECTS

• A *retained object* is an object that has been retained after the verb has been changed from the active voice to the passive voice.

Example:

a. Jesus gave the twelve apostles some encouragement. (*Encouragement* is the direct object of the verb *gave.*)

Now arrange the sentence with the verb in the passive voice. See page 104.

b. The twelve apostles were given encouragement by Jesus. (*Encouragement* has been retained as an object.)

EXERCISE 18

In the following sentences write O.C. above the objective complement and R.O. above the retained object.

1. Jesus must have considered the apostles faithful men.
2. Reading the Bible makes men wise.
3. The disciples told the multitudes truths about the Lord.
4. The multitudes were told truths about the Lord.
5. Christ can make a sinner whole.

EXPLORING TRUTHS

I. Choose a noun, such as life, death, truth, beauty, covenant, etc., and find at least ten Bible references using your noun. Does the noun always mean the same thing? Do you find any differences in the usage in different books? In the Old Testament and the New Testament? In the same book of the Bible?

II. In reading a book in the Bible, find a noun which is repeated many times. This is a good way to find the theme of a book.

Example: truth — II Timothy

TEST ON CHAPTER 9

I. Name 8 different ways in which a noun can be used.

1.
2.
3.
4.
5.
6.
7.
8.

II. Tell how the noun *basket* is used in each of the following sentences. Is it a subject, direct object, indirect object, predicate nominative, object of preposition, appostive, possessive, or noun of direct address?

1. Put a ribbon on the *basket.* __________
2. A little boy brought the *basket* to Jesus. __________
3. The *basket* contained fish. __________
4. The *basket's* contents were enjoyed by all. __________
5. His mother made the *basket* a handle. __________
6. Mr. *Basket,* do you know how important you are? __________
7. The container, a brown *basket,* was never preserved for a museum. __________
8. That is a *basket* that became famous. __________

III. Tell how each underlined noun is used in the following sentences.

1. Enter in at the straight *gate.* __________
2. Wide is the *gate* and broad is the *way* that leads to destruction. __________ __________
3. Straight is the gate and narrow is the way which leads to *life.* __________
4. Few there be that find that *gate.* __________
5. Beware of false prophets which come in *sheep's* clothing. __________
6. *Lord,* in your name we cast out devils. __________
7. A wise man is a *person* who listens to *God's* Word and obeys it. __________ __________
8. A disobedient man, a foolish *person,* chooses to separate himself from God. __________

CHAPTER 10

MORE LEARNING ABOUT PRONOUNS

In Chapter 2 the three cases of pronouns—the nominative, the objective, and the possessive—were discussed. Now it is important to apply these cases and use pronouns correctly. The misuse of pronouns is a very common practice. Study the following sentences containing the first person, singular pronoun.

1. *I* must obey the commandments in the Bible. (*I* is the subject of the verb must obey.)
2. It is *I* who should be thankful. (*I* is a predicate nominative.)
3. Christ saved *me* from the consequences of sin. (*Me* is used as the direct object of the verb saved.)
4. The Lord gave *me* the responsibility of reaching others with the truth of salvation. (*Me* is used as the indirect object of the verb gave.)
5. Christ died for *me.* (*Me* is used as the object of the preposition for.)
6. The redeemed ones, you and *I,* are bought with a price, the precious blood of Jesus Christ. (*I* is used as an appositive.)

LESSON 10-A USING PRONOUNS AS SUBJECTS

● *Pronouns* used as *subjects of verbs* are always in the nominative case. Remember that the subject of a sentence is a word or group of words which names the person, place, thing, or idea about which something is said.

Examples:

a. Mom, Dad, and I (not me) go to Sunday School.
b. We three enjoy our classes. (not us)

In sentences *a* and *b,* the pronouns *I* and *we* are used as subjects of the verbs.

NOTE: In some sentences, the 2nd person singular and 2nd person plural pronouns, *you,* is omitted. However, most English speaking people understand what is meant.

Examples:

a. Repent and be baptized. (The subject *you* is understood.)
b. Grieve not the Holy Spirit. (What is the subject of the sentence? *You* is understood to be the subject.)

EXERCISE 1

Review the nominative pronouns by writing them in the space provided. If you have forgotten them, look back to page 18.

	Singular	Plural
1st person		
2nd person		
3rd person		

EXERCISE 2

Circle the nominative pronouns used as subjects in the following sentences.

1. In Sunday School (we, us) learn about God.
2. Sometimes the teacher lectures and other times (he or she) (him or her) dramatizes the lesson.
3. My brother and (I, me) enjoy our classes.
4. My sister and (she, her) play school at home.
5. All of the children stop for a drink at the water fountain and (they, them) remember that Christ is the water of life.
6. Many times (we, us) children learn verses.

NOTE: In compound subjects, be certain to put the last mentioned subject in the nominative case.

LESSON 10-B USING PRONOUNS AS PREDICATE NOMINATIVES

● *Pronouns used as predicate nominatives* (subject complements) must always be in the nominative case. Remember that a *predicate nominative* is a pronoun, noun, or adjective which follows a linking verb and refers to the subject.

EXERCISE 3

Write as many linking verbs as you can in the space provided. Refer to page 28 if you have forgotten the linking verbs.

EXERCISE 4

Circle the nominative pronouns, used as predicate nominatives, in the following sentences.

1. And even to your old age, I am (he, him) who will carry you. (Isaiah 46:4)
2. Therefore they shall know in that day that I am (he, him) that does speak; behold, it is (I, me). (Isaiah 52:9)
3. They on the rock are (they, them), which, when they hear, receive the word with joy. (Luke 8:13)

4. Could it have been (we, us) who completed the memorization projects so well?
5. It is (she, her) who chose to study the Bible.
6. Some said, This is (he, him): others said, He is like him: but he said, I am (he, him). (John 9:9)
7. It is (he, him) that sitteth upon the circle of the earth, and the inhabitants thereof are as grasshoppers. (Isaiah 40:22)
8. But you are (they, them) that forsake the Lord. (Isaiah 65:11)

LESSON 10-C USING PRONOUNS AS DIRECT OBJECTS

• *Pronouns* used as *direct objects* must always be in the objective case. Remember that a *direct object* is a noun or pronoun which receives the action of the verb and answers the questions *what* or *whom.*

EXERCISE 5

Review the objective pronouns by writing them in the space provided. If you have forgotten them, look back to page 18.

	Singular	Plural
1st person		
2nd person		
3rd person		

EXERCISE 6

Circle the objective pronouns used as direct object in the following sentences.

1. Here am I; send me. (Isaiah 6:8)
2. God has predestinated us unto the adoption of children by Jesus Christ to himself. (Ephesians 1:5)
3. But God, who is rich in mercy, for his great love wherewith he loved us,
4. Even when we were dead in sins, has quickened us together with Christ, (by grace you are saved),
5. And has raised us up together, and made us sit in heavenly places in Christ Jesus. (Ephesians 2:4-6)

LESSON 10-D USING PRONOUNS AS INDIRECT OBJECTS

• *Pronouns* used as *indirect objects* must always be in the objective case. Remember that an indirect object is a noun or pronoun that answers the questions *to whom* or *for what* something is done.

EXERCISE 7

Underline the pronouns used as indirect objects in the following sentences.

1. God has given us all spiritual blessings in Christ.
2. He has told you and me the mystery of his will that we should be to the praise of his glory.
3. Are you aware that God will grant you power through his Holy Spirit?

LESSON 10-E USING PRONOUNS AS OBJECTS OF THE PREPOSITION

● *Pronouns* which follow prepositions and serve as objects of the preposition must always be in the objective case.

EXERCISE 8

Circle the pronouns used as objects of the prepositions in the following sentences.

1. For he is our peace, who has made both one, and has broken down the middle wall of partition between us. (Ephesians 2:14)
2. "Look unto me, and be saved," said the Lord.
3. For to me to live is Christ. (Philippians 1:21)
4. Let this mind be in you, which was also in Christ Jesus. (Philippians 2:5)
5. By him were all things created. (Colossians 1:16)

LESSON 10-F USING PRONOUNS AS APPOSITIVES

● If the *pronoun used as an appositive* stands next to a noun used as a subject, then the pronoun must be in the nominative case. If the *pronoun used as an appositive* stands next to a noun used as an object, then the pronoun must be in the objective case.

Examples:

a. The students, *you* and *I*, studied hard. (The pronouns are nominative because students is the subject of the sentence).
b. I gave a test to the best students, *him* and *her*. (Students is used as an object of the preposition to; therefore, the pronouns in apposition must be in the objective case).

EXERCISE 9

Circle the correct pronouns in the following sentences.

1. No matter how you consider the situation, it was (he, him) whom they opposed.
2. Everybody passed the memorization contest except Mike and (I, me).

3. It must have been (they, them).
4. Between you and (her, she) there is no difference.
5. It is a good thing for you and (I, me) to tithe.
6. (We, us) young people should assist the older people.
7. The older people should pray for (us, we) young folks.
8. It was always (she, her) who sang the solo part.
9. If I were (she, her), I would practice daily.
10. The leader asked (I, me) rather than (him, he) to play.

EXERCISE 10

Here are some sentences to work on.

1. The missionary society chose three candidates, Henry, Tom, and (I, me).
2. The pastor said that it was (they, them) who deserved to go to India.
3. The church gave (us, we) three the money to go.
4. I knew it would be (them, they) who would go.
5. Henry, Tom, and (I, me) prayed hard about the idea.
6. (We, us) three wanted to serve God.
7. Now the three of (we, us) must study a new language.
8. This opportunity is (our's, ours).
9. The young people (theirselves, themselves) must raise support.
10. Henry will get his own support by (hisself, himself), but Tom and (I, me) will get help from our parents.

LESSON 10-G USING WHO AND WHOM CORRECTLY

• There are two interrogative pronouns, *who* and *whom,* which are often used incorrectly.

Who is the nominative form of the pronoun and is used when a subject of the verb or a predicate pronoun is needed.

Whom is the objective form of the pronoun and is used when a direct object, an indirect object, or an object of the preposition is needed.

Examples:

a. *Who* sent the apostles forth to heal the sick, cleanse the lepers, and do good deeds? (*Who* is the subject of the sentence.)
b. *Whom* should they fear? (*Whom* is the direct object of the verb should fear.)

EXERCISE 11

Select the correct form of who or whom in the following sentences. Many times the Bible uses the word *whosoever* for who and *whomsoever* for whom.

1. (Whosoever, whomsoever) shall confess me before men, him will I confess also before my Father which is in heaven. (Matthew 10:32)
2. (Who, Whom) has ears to hear, let him hear. (Matthew 13:9)
3. Blessed is the man (who, whom) God chooses. (Psalm 65:4)
4. For (who, whom) in heaven can be compared unto the Lord. (Psalm 89:6)
5. Blessed is the man (who, whom) you chasten, O Lord. (Psalm 94:12)

EXPLORING TRUTHS

Read Colossians 2. Then make 2 lists. In the first list, write some of the admonitions, reminders, or exhortations that Paul gives to you. In the second list, place all of the qualities, characteristics, or promises of God, the Father; Jesus, the Son; and the Holy Spirit, the Comforter.

TEST ON CHAPTER 10

I. Name the three cases of personal pronouns in the English language.
   1.
   2.
   3.

II. Write the nominative pronouns.

III. Write the objective pronouns.

IV. Write the possessive pronouns.

V. In the space at the right tell what *case* is used in each underlined pronoun.

1. When (a) he (Jesus) came down from the mountain, great multitudes followed (b) him.
2. A leper came and worshipped him, saying "Lord, if (c) you will, you can make (d) me whole."
3. Jesus said, "Go (e) your way and tell no one. Take your gift and offer (f) it to the priest."

from Matthew 8:1-4

4. Both (g) he and (h) I should thank God for (i) his grace to us.
5. (j) We Christians should have rejoicing hearts.

a. ____________
b. ____________
c. ____________
d. ____________
e. ____________
f. ____________
g. ____________
h. ____________
i. ____________
j. ____________

VI. Name 5 different types of pronouns and give an example of each.

	Type	Example
1.	____________	____________
2.	____________	____________
3.	____________	____________
4.	____________	____________
5.	____________	____________

VII. Which kinds of pronouns

1. ask a question? ____________
2. show 3 persons? ____________
3. use *'s* to show possession? ____________
4. show number? ____________
5. point out persons or things? ____________
6. show gender? ____________
7. add *self* or *selves* to make the pronoun? ____________
8. do not take apostrophes? ____________

VIII. Underline the pronouns in the following sentences. In the spaces at the right tell the kinds of pronoun underlined. For each personal pronoun, tell how that is used. The first one has been done for you.

Sentence		Kind	Usage
1. I know that you can do every thing.	a.	personal	subject
	b.	relative	______
	c.	personal	subject
2. Who is he that hides counsel without knowledge?	d.	______	______
	e.	______	______
	f.	______	______
3. Therefore have I uttered that I understood not	g.	______	______
	h.	______	______
	i.	______	______
4. I have heard of you by the hearing of the ear, but now my eye sees you.	j.	______	______
	k.	______	______
	l.	______	______
	m.	______	______
5. Wherefore, I abhor myself and repent in dust and ashes. from Job 42:2-6	n.	______	______
	o.	______	______

CHAPTER 11

MORE LEARNING ABOUT VERBS

In Chapter 3 you learned that verbs are words that show action or state of being. You also learned that verbs may consist of more than one word, called a verb phrase. Now think about another characteristic of verbs. Verbs are highly inflected; that is, they have more than one form to show time.

- *Tense* is the term used to express distinctions in time. In the English language there are six tenses: the present tense, the past tense, the future tense, the present perfect tense, the past perfect tense, and the future perfect tense. These tenses are formed from the *principal parts of verbs.*

LESSON 11-A LEARNING THE PRINCIPAL PARTS OF VERBS

- The *principal parts* of a verb are the present infinitive, the present participle, the past (first person singular), and the past participle. (Some grammarians list a fifth principal part called the third person, singular form.)

Examples:

PRESENT	PRESENT PARTICIPLE	PAST	PAST PARTICIPLE
talk	talking	talked	(has) talked
work	working	worked	(has) worked
eat	eating	ate	(has) eaten
go	going	went	(has) gone

- To form principal parts of verbs, it is necessary to know the difference between *regular verbs* and *irregular verbs.*

A *regular verb* is one which forms its past and past participle forms by adding -ed, or -d to the present form. See *talk* and *work* above.

An *irregular verb* is one which forms its past and past participle forms in an irregular way. See *eat* and *go* above.

Listed below are some *irregular verbs* with their principal parts. Try to memorize the parts if you do not know them. In order to form tenses correctly, you must know the principal parts of verbs.

PRESENT	PRESENT PARTICIPLE	PAST	PAST PARTICIPLE
am	being	was	(has) been
arise	arising	arose	(has) arisen
awake	awaking	awoke	(has) awaked
bear	bearing	bore	(has) borne
beat	beating	beat	(has) beaten
become	becoming	became	(has) become
begin	beginning	began	(has) begun
bend	bending	bent	(has) bent
bite	biting	bit	(has) bitten

PRESENT	PRESENT PARTICIPLE	PAST	PAST PARTICIPLE
blow	blowing	blew	(has) blown
break	breaking	broke	(has) broken
bring	bringing	brought	(has) brought
catch	catching	caught	(has) caught
choose	choosing	chose	(has) chosen
come	coming	came	(has) come
dig	digging	dug	(has) dug
do	doing	did	(has) done
draw	drawing	drew	(has) drawn
drink	drinking	drank	(has) drunk
drive	driving	drove	(has) driven
eat	eating	ate	(has) eaten
fall	falling	fell	(has) fallen
fly	flying	flew	(has) flown
freeze	freezing	froze	(has) frozen
give	giving	gave	(has) given
go	going	went	(has) gone
grow	growing	grew	(has) grown
hang (suspend)	hanging	hung	(has) hung
hang (execute)	hanging	hanged	(has) hanged
hear	hearing	heard	(has) heard
hide	hiding	hid	(has) hidden
hurt	hurting	hurt	(has) hurt
know	knowing	knew	(has) known
lay (to put)	laying	laid	(has) laid
lead	leading	led	(has) led
lend	lending	lent	(has) lent
lie (to rest)	lying	lay	(has) lain
lie (to tell lies)	lying	lied	(has) lied
lose	losing	lost	(has) lost
prove	proving	proved	(has) proven
read	reading	read	(has) read
ride	riding	rode	(has) ridden
ring	ringing	rang	(has) rung
rise	rising	rose	(has) risen
run	running	ran	(has) run
say	saying	said	(has) said
see	seeing	saw	(has) seen
set	setting	set	(has) set
shake	shaking	shook	(has) shaken
shine	shining	shone	(has) shone
sing	singing	sang	(has) sung
sit	sitting	sat	(has) sat
slay	slaying	slew	(has) slain
speak	speaking	spoke	(has) spoken
spring	springing	sprang	(has) sprung
steal	stealing	stole	(has) stolen
swim	swimming	swam	(has) swum
take	taking	took	(has) taken

PRESENT	PRESENT PARTICIPLE	PAST	PAST PARTICIPLE
teach	teaching	taught	(has) taught
tear	tearing	tore	(has) torn
throw	throwing	threw	(has) thrown
write	writing	wrote	(has) written

When you are in doubt about the forms of a verb, be certain to use your dictionary to find the correct spelling and pronunciation of the words.

EXERCISE 1

In the space at the right, tell whether the verbs are regular verbs or irregular verbs.

1. begin ____________
2. behold ____________
3. burn ____________
4. forgive ____________
5. play ____________
6. kneel ____________
7. cry ____________
8. pass ____________
9. create ____________
10. raise ____________

EXERCISE 2

Now fill in the blanks below and see if you know the principal parts of the above verbs. Use your dictionary if it is necessary.

PRESENT	PRESENT PARTICIPLE	PAST	PAST PARTICIPLE
1. begin			
2.	beholding		
3.		burned	
4.			have forgiven
5.	playing		
6. kneel			
7.			have cried
8.		passed	
9. create			
10.	raising		

LESSON 11-B LEARNING ABOUT THE PRESENT TENSE

● Now consider the formation of the six tenses. The *present tense* indicates something that is happening now. It is usually formed from the infinitive, the form of the verb usually preceded by the word *to*. The third person, singular, present form always adds *-s* or *-es* to the stem of the verb. You learned about person and number in Chapter 2, pp. 17 and 18.

PRESENT TENSE

	Singular	Plural
1st person	I talk	we talk
2nd person	you talk	you talk
3rd person	he, she, it talks	they talk

EXERCISE 3

Write the present tense of the verb *work.*

	Singular	Plural
1st person		
2nd person		
3rd person		

EXERCISE 4

Write the present tense of the verb *eat.*

	Singular	Plural
1st person		
2nd person		
3rd person		

LESSON 11-C LEARNING ABOUT THE PAST TENSE

- The *past tense* indicates something that happened in the past. With a regular verb, the addition of *-d* or *-ed* to the stem of the verb indicates past time. Irregular verbs change their past tense in many ways. Look again at the variety of ways in which verbs form past tenses. See pages 91 and 92.

PAST TENSE — Regular Verb

	Singular	Plural
1st person	I talked	we talked
2nd person	you talked	you talked
3rd person	he, she, it talked	they talked

PAST TENSE — Irregular Verb

	Singular	Plural
1st person	I ate	we ate
2nd person	you ate	you ate
3rd person	he, she, it ate	they ate

EXERCISE 5

Write the past tense of the verb *work.*

	Singular	Plural
1st person		
2nd person		
3rd person		

EXERCISE 6

Write the past tense of the verb *go.*

	Singular	Plural
1st person		
2nd person		
3rd person		

Many errors are made in the use of the past tense. Little children are aware that past time is indicated by the addition of *-ed* to a verb. Frequently, those who use substandard English will say:

I *felled* from the tree.
Or, he *throwed* the ball.
Or, we *knowed* the answer.

Another error is made when the past participle is used incorrectly.

I *done* my homework.
They *seen* the plane in the sky.
She *brung* the book to class.

EXERCISE 7

Cross out the incorrect form of the verb in the following sentences and write the correct form in the space at the right.

1. The child felled from the tree. ______________
2. He throwed the ball. ______________
3. We knowed the answer. ______________
4. I done my homework. ______________
5. They seen the plane in the sky. ______________
6. She brung the book to class. ______________

LESSON 11-D LEARNING ABOUT TENSE CONSISTENCY.

- Writers and speakers of the English language must be careful about *tense consistency.* Be careful not to switch back and forth between the present and the past tenses in the same sentence or the same paragraph.

Example:

When Jesus was entered into Capernaum, there *comes* unto him a centurion who *has* a sick servant. Jesus said that he would heal the man. The centurion *answers* that he *is* not worthy. He told Jesus to speak the word only and his servant would be healed. When Jesus *hears* that, he marvelled and *says*, "Verily I say unto you, I have not found so great faith, no, not in Israel."

The underlined verbs in the above paragraph should be in the past tense. Notice how much better the paragraph reads when *tense consistency* is applied.

When Jesus was entered into Capernaum, there *came* unto him a centurion who *had* a sick servant. Jesus said that he would heal the man. The centurion *answered* that he *was* not worthy. He told Jesus to speak the word only and his servant would be healed. When Jesus *heard* that, he marvelled and *said*, "Verily I say unto you, I have not found so great faith, no, not in Israel."

from Matthew 8:5-10

EXERCISE 8

In the following sentences, the underlined verbs are in the wrong tense. In the space at the right, write the correct verb form.

1. When Jesus was entered into a ship, his disciples follow him. __________
2. Behold, there arose a great tempest in the sea, insomuch that the ship is covered. __________
3. Jesus was asleep, and his disciples come to him, and awoke him, saying, "Lord, save us; we perish." __________
4. Jesus says unto them, "Why are you so fearful, O you of little faith?" __________

from Matthew 8:23-26

LESSON 11-E LEARNING ABOUT THE FUTURE TENSE

• The *future tense* is used to express something that will happen at a later time. To form the future tense of a verb, you must add the auxiliary verbs *shall* and *will* to the stem of the verb.

FUTURE TENSE

	Singular	Plural
1st person	I shall talk	we shall talk
2nd person	you will talk	you will talk
3rd person	he, she, it will talk	they will talk

EXERCISE 9

Write the future tense of the verb *work.*

	Singular	Plural
1st person		
2nd person		
3rd person		

EXERCISE 10

Write the future tense of the verb *eat.*

	Singular	Plural
1st person		
2nd person		
3rd person		

- In informal English the word *will* is used in the first person singular and plural forms.

Example:

I will talk	we will talk

- In formal English, the word *shall* is used in the first person singular and plural forms. However, when the future tense is used to express determination or promise, *shall* and *will* are used in the opposite positions.

Example:

I will talk	we will talk
you shall talk	you shall talk
he, she, it shall talk	they shall talk

The Bible contains many promises and warnings, and the use of *will* and *shall* places emphasis on these blessings and admonitions.

Example:

They that wait upon the Lord *shall* renew their strength; they *shall* mount up with wings as eagles; they *shall* run, and not be weary; and they *shall* walk, and not faint.

Isaiah 40:31

If the writer had not wanted to stress the promises, he would have used the plain future form and changed *shall* to *will.*

EXERCISE 11

In the following sentences make a choice between *shall* and *will.* Read the scripture verses if you have any doubts about the form of the verb. Write *shall* or *will* in the space at the right, and then write *F* for plain future tense, *D* for determination, and *P* for promise.

1. Fear thou not; for I am with thee; be not dismayed; for I am thy God; I (shall, will) strengthen thee. (Isaiah 41:10) ______ ______
2. Even the youths (shall, will) faint and be weary, ______ ______ and the young men (shall, will) utterly fall. ______ ______ (Isaiah 40:30)
3. The Lord is my shepherd; I (shall, will) not want. ______ ______ (Psalm 23:1)
4. Yea, though I walk through the valley of the shadow of death, I (shall, will) fear no evil. ______ ______ (Psalm 23:4)
5. For the Lord himself (shall, will) descend from ______ ______ heaven with a shout, with the voice of the archangel, and with the trump of God; and the dead in Christ (shall, will) rise first. ______ ______ (I Thessalonians 4:16)
6. And I (will, shall) come near to you to judgment; ______ ______ and I (shall, will) be a swift witness against the ______ ______ sorcerers, and against the adulterers, and against false swearers, and against those that oppress the hireling in *his* wages the widow, and the fatherless, and that turn aside the stranger *from his right,* and fear not me, saith the Lord of hosts. (Malachi 3:5)

EXERCISE 12

In the space at the right, tell what tense the underlined verb expresses. Is it present, past, or future tense?

1. Neither <u>*is*</u> there salvation in any other; for there is none other name under heaven given among men, whereby we must be saved. (Acts 4:12) ____________
2. But we <u>*will give*</u> ourselves continually to prayer, and to the ministry of the word. (Acts 6:4) ____________
3. And they *said,* "Believe on the Lord Jesus Christ and you <u>*shall be saved*</u> and your house." ____________ (Acts 16:31)

4. For in him we *live*, and *move*, and have our being. (Acts 17:28) ____________

5. And some *believed* the things which were spoken, and some believed not. (Acts 28:24) ____________

EXERCISE 13

Write the correct form of the verb to agree with the subjects listed below.

1. I	(present of believe)	____________
2. You	(past of believe)	____________
3. He	(future of believe)	____________
4. We	(present of hope)	____________
5. You	(past of hope)	____________
6. They	(future of hope)	____________

LESSON 11-F LEARNING THE PRESENT PERFECT TENSE

● The *present perfect tense* refers to an action which was started in the past but has been completed in the present. Two auxiliary verbs, *has* and *have*, are added to the past participle of a verb to form the present perfect tense.

PRESENT PERFECT TENSE

	Singular	Plural
1st person	I have talked	we have talked
2nd person	you have talked	you have talked
3rd person	he, she, it has talked	they have talked

EXERCISE 14

Write the present perfect tense of the verb *work*.

	Singular	Plural
1st person		
2nd person		
3rd person		

EXERCISE 15

Write the present perfect tense of the verb *eat*.

	Singular	Plural
1st person		
2nd person		
3rd person		

LESSON 11-G LEARNING THE PAST PERFECT TENSE

● The *past perfect tense* indicates action completed in the past before some other action had happened in the past. The auxiliary *had* is added to the past participle of the verb to form the past perfect tense.

PAST PERFECT TENSE

	Singular	Plural
1st person	I had talked	we had talked
2nd person	you had talked	you had talked
3rd person	he, she, it had talked	they had talked

EXERCISE 16

Write the past perfect tense of the verb *work.*

	Singular	Plural
1st person		
2nd person		
3rd person		

EXERCISE 17

Write the past perfect tense of the verb *eat.*

	Singular	Plural
1st person		
2nd person		
3rd person		

LESSON 11-H LEARNING THE FUTURE PERFECT TENSE

● The *future perfect tense* indicates action that will be completed in the future before some other action occurs. The auxiliary verbs *shall have* or *will have* are added to the past participle of the verb to form the future perfect tense.

FUTURE PERFECT TENSE

	Singular	Plural
1st person	I shall have talked	we shall have talked
2nd person	you will have talked	you will have talked
3rd person	he, she, it will have talked	they will have talked

EXERCISE 18

Write the future perfect tense of the verb *work.*

	Singular	Plural
1st person		
2nd person		
3rd person		

EXERCISE 19

Write the future perfect tense of the verb *eat.*

	Singular	Plural
1st person		
2nd person		
3rd person		

EXERCISE 20

What tense is shown in each of the following sentences?

Example:

a. I go. — present
b. They had gone. — past perfect

1. She believes. ______
2. They respected. ______
3. We shall have seen. ______
4. You asked. ______
5. I have heard. ______
6. The rain descended. ______
7. The floods will come. ______
8. Jesus had spoken. ______
9. We taught. ______
10. They had known. ______

LESSON 11-I LEARNING THE PROGRESSIVE AND EMPHATIC FORMS OF VERBS

● There are two other forms of verbs called the *progressive form* and the *emphatic form.* The progressive form uses the present participle (the *-ing* form) and a form of the verb *be.* The emphatic form uses the present stem and a form of the verb *do.* When all forms of a verb are given in proper order, a *conjugation* is completed.

Here is a chart which gives a conjugation in three forms.

CONJUGATION OF TALK

Principal parts: talk, talking, talked, have talked

TENSE	(INDICATIVE) COMMON	PROGRESSIVE	EMPHATIC
PRESENT	I talk you talk he talks	I am talking you are talking he is talking	I do talk you do talk he does talk
	we talk you talk they talk	we are talking you are talking they are talking	we do talk you do talk they do talk
PAST	I talked you talked he talked	I was talking you were talking he was talking	I did talk you did talk he did talk
	we talked you talked they talked	we were talking you were talking they were talking	we did talk you did talk they did talk
FUTURE	I shall talk you will talk he will talk	I shall be talking you will be talking he will be talking	
	we shall talk you will talk they will talk	we shall be talking you will be talking they will be talking	
PRESENT PERFECT	I have talked you have talked he has talked	I have been talking you have been talking he has been talking	
	we have talked you have talked they have talked	we have been talking you have been talking they have been talking	
PAST PERFECT	I had talked you had talked he had talked	I had been talking you had been talking he had been talking	
	we had talked you had talked they had talked	we had been talking you had been talking they had been talking	

FUTURE PERFECT	I shall have talked	I shall have been talking
	you will have talked	you will have been talking
	he will have talked	he will have been talking
	we shall have talked	we shall have been talking
	you will have talked	you will have been talking
	they will have talked	they will have been talking

NOTE: There is no emphatic form in the future or perfect tenses. However, determination or emphasis is shown in the future tense by changing the positions of *shall* and *will.* See pages 97 and 98.

EXERCISE 21

Write a *conjugation* of the verb *love* in the *active voice, indicative mood,* in all 6 tenses in the space provided.

CONJUGATION — ACTIVE VOICE

PRESENT TENSE

Singular	Plural
______________________	______________________
______________________	______________________
______________________	______________________

PAST TENSE

______________________	______________________
______________________	______________________
______________________	______________________

FUTURE TENSE

______________________	______________________
______________________	______________________
______________________	______________________

PRESENT PERFECT TENSE

______________________	______________________
______________________	______________________
______________________	______________________

PAST PERFECT TENSE

______________________	______________________
______________________	______________________
______________________	______________________

FUTURE PERFECT TENSE

______________________ ______________________

______________________ ______________________

______________________ ______________________

LESSON 11-J LEARNING ABOUT VOICE

- Another characteristic of verbs is that they have *voice.* A verb in the *active voice* has a subject which is the doer of the action. All of the conjugations given above have been in the active voice.
- A verb in the *passive voice* has its subject being acted upon.

Examples:

Active voice: Jesus *healed* the woman.
Passive voice: The woman *was healed* by Jesus.

In the first sentence the verb is in the active voice because the subject Jesus is the doer of the action. In the second sentence, the receiver of the action has become the subject, and the verb is in the passive voice.

The active voice is a more forceful way of speaking and is used more frequently than the passive voice. Many times newspapers use the passive voice.

Example:

It *was reported* that the translation was made by a Greek scholar.

EXERCISE 22

Tell whether the underlined verbs in the sentences below are in the active voice or the passive voice.

1. In the evening, the people *brought* many that *were possessed* to Jesus. __________ __________
2. Jesus cast out the spirits with his Word, and many *were healed.* __________ __________
3. When Jesus *entered* into a ship, his disciples *followed* him. __________ __________
4. The ship *arrived* at Capernaum. __________
5. A man sick of the palsy was *brought* to Jesus. __________
6. When Jesus saw the faith of the man, he *forgave* his sins and *healed* him. __________ __________ __________

from Matthew 9:1-3

• The *passive voice* of a verb is formed by using the verb *be* and the past participle of the verb. Here is a conjugation in the passive voice.

CONJUGATION — PASSIVE VOICE

PRESENT TENSE

Singular	Plural
I am covered	we are covered
you are covered	you are covered
he, she, it is covered	they are covered

PAST TENSE

Singular	Plural
I was covered	we were covered
you were covered	you were covered
he, she, it was covered	they were covered

FUTURE TENSE

Singular	Plural
I shall be covered	we shall be covered
you will be covered	you will be covered
he, she, it will be covered	they will be covered

PRESENT PERFECT TENSE

Singular	Plural
I have been covered	we have been covered
you have been covered	you had been covered
he, she, it has been covered	they have been covered

PAST PERFECT TENSE

Singular	Plural
I had been covered	we had been covered
you had been covered	you had been covered
he, she, it had been covered	they had been covered

FUTURE PERFECT TENSE

Singular	Plural
I shall have been covered	we shall have been covered
you will have been covered	you will have been covered
he, she, it will have been covered	they will have been covered

If you have a need for a progressive form of the passive voice, add *being* to each form.

Example:

I *am being* covered.
I *was being* covered.

EXERCISE 23

In the space provided, write a *conjugation* of the verb *love in the passive voice* in all 6 tenses.

PRESENT TENSE

Singular	Plural
__________	__________
__________	__________
__________	__________

PAST TENSE

FUTURE TENSE

PRESENT PERFECT TENSE

PAST PERFECT TENSE

FUTURE PERFECT TENSE

LESSON 11-K LEARNING ABOUT MOOD

- There are three moods, or modes, of verbs. The *indicative mood* makes a statement or asks a question. All that has been said about verbs in this chapter has been in the indicative mood.
- Another mood is the *imperative mood.* The imperative mood makes a command or a request.
- The *subjunctive mood* expresses a statement contrary to fact, a wish, an exhortation, a requirement, or a motion or resolution.

Examples:

1. Indicative mood
   The fruit of the Spirit *is* in all goodness and righteousness and truth. (Ephesians 5:9)
2. Imperative mood
   Don't give place to the devil. (Ephesians 4:27)
3. Subjunctive mood
   a. If I *were* Martha, I would have also sat at Jesus' feet. (Contrary to fact)
   b. I wish that I *were* older. (A wish)
   c. Be not drunk with wine, where is excess; but *be* filled with the Spirit. (An exhortation) (Ephesians 5:18)
   d. Resolved, that these issues be studied. (A resolution)
   e. It is necessary that he do his assignments daily. (A requirement)

In formal English, the use of the subjunctive mood is observed. Generally speaking, the indicative mood is used in America.

To form the subjunctive mood, you conjugate the verb (except the verb *be*) exactly as in the indicative mood, except for the third person singular, present tense. No *-s* is added to this form in the subjunctive mood. Study the chart below.

PRESENT TENSE

Indicative		Subjunctive	
I do	we do	I do	we do
you do	you do	you do	you do
he, she, it does	they do	he, she, it do	they do

PRESENT TENSE OF BE

I am	we are	I be	we be
you are	you are	you be	you be
he, she it is	they are	he, she, it be	they be

PAST TENSE OF BE

I was	we were	I were	we were
you were	you were	you were	you were
he, she, it was	they were	he, she, it were	they were

EXERCISE 24

Select the correct verb form for *formal* English.

1. I move that the budget (is, be, was) accepted. ________
2. The student acted as if he (was, were) the teacher. ________
3. I suggest that you (be, are) quiet in church. ________
4. God (forbid, forbids) that I should boast. ________
5. If I (was, were) you, I would study harder. ________

EXPLORING TRUTHS

Read the books of I and II Timothy. Notice the transitive verbs in the active voice which are used. Words such as *charge, commit, exhort,* and *give* are used. What effect do these verbs have on your life? Make a list of the things which Paul urges Christians to do, and then decide how you can make your Christian life more used of God.

TEST ON CHAPTER 11

I. The four principal parts of a verb are called:

1.
2.
3.
4.

II. A regular verb is one which forms its past tense by adding ______ or ______.

III. Verbs which indicate their past tense by changing the form of the verb are called:

______________________.

IV. Write the principal parts of the following verbs:

1. do	______	______	______
2. read	______	______	______

V. Give a conjugation in the active voice in all six tenses of the verb *be.*

PRESENT TENSE

Singular	Plural
______	______
______	______
______	______

PAST TENSE

Singular	Plural
______	______
______	______
______	______

FUTURE TENSE

Singular	Plural
______	______
______	______
______	______

PRESENT PERFECT TENSE

Singular	Plural
______	______
______	______
______	______

PAST PERFECT TENSE

Singular	Plural
____________________	____________________
____________________	____________________
____________________	____________________

FUTURE PERFECT TENSE

Singular	Plural
____________________	____________________
____________________	____________________
____________________	____________________

VI. Fill in the blanks in the following sentences.

1. A verb which has a subject that is the doer of the action is in the __________ voice.
2. A verb which has a subject which is the receiver of the action is in the ________ voice.
3. The first person, singular, present tense, progressive form of the verb *bring* is ______________________________.
4. The third person, plural, past tense, emphatic form of the verb *bring* is ______________________________.
5. The first person, plural, future tense, passive voice form of the verb *bring* is ______________________________.

VII. The three moods of verbs in the English are the ________________, ________________, and ________________.

CHAPTER 12

MORE LEARNING ABOUT ADJECTIVES

In Chapter 4 you learned that adjectives are words which modify nouns or pronouns. You also learned that there are two broad kinds of adjectives, descriptive adjectives and limiting adjectives. Now turn your attention to *predicate adjectives.*

LESSON 12-A LEARNING ABOUT PREDICATE ADJECTIVES

- A *predicate adjective* is an adjective that follows a linking verb and completes the meaning of the subject. Refer to page 28 if you have forgotten the linking verbs. Predicate adjectives are also known as predicate nominatives or subject complements.

Example:

The ruler in Matthew 9 said, "Master, my daughter is *dead*." (*Dead* is the predicate adjective because it describes the subject's daughter.)

EXERCISE 1

List at least 10 verbs which can be used as linking verbs.

1.	6.
2.	7.
3.	8.
4.	9.
5.	10.

EXERCISE 2

Underline the predicate adjectives in the following sentences.

1. The foolishness of God is wiser than men.
2. And the weakness of God is stronger than men. (I Corinthians 2:25)
3. All people are precious in God's sight.
4. Paul was gentle among the people. (I Thessalonians 2:7)
5. The Thessalonians were dear to him. (I Thessalonians 2:8)

NOTE: Use adjectives after such linking verbs as *be, look, taste, smell, feel, sound, appear, seem, grow,* and *become* when the adjectives qualify the subject.

Examples:

a. I feel bad (not badly). Bad modifies I.
b. The candy tastes sweet (not sweetly). Sweet modifies candy.

EXERCISE 3

In the space at the right, tell whether the underlined words are predicate nouns, predicate pronouns, or predicate adjectives. One sentence has no predicate nominative.

1. Be not *wise* in your own eyes: fear the Lord. ____________
2. It shall be *health* to your navel and *marrow* to your bones. ____________ ____________
3. Despise not the chastening of the Lord; neither be *weary* of his correction. ____________
4. Happy is the *man* that finds wisdom. ____________
5. For the merchandise of it is *better* than the merchandise of silver. ____________
6. She is more *precious* than rubies. ____________
7. Length of days is in her right hand; and in her left hand are *riches* and *honour.* ____________ ____________
8. Her ways are *ways* of pleasantness, and all paths are peace. ____________
9. The one who finds wisdom is *he* who finds God. ____________

from Proverbs 3

LESSON 12-B LEARNING ABOUT DEGREES OF COMPARISON

● Another characteristic of adjectives is that they can show comparison. Most adjectives have three degrees of comparison: the *positive,* the *comparative,* and the *superlative.*

The *positive* degree names a quality.

Example:

Zaccheus was a *short* man.

The *comparative* degree is used in comparing two persons or things.

Example:

Zaccheus was *shorter* than James.

The *superlative* degree is used in comparing more than two persons or things.

Example:

Zaccheus was the *shortest* man in the crowd.

Almost all adjectives of one syllable form their comparative degree by adding *-r* or *-er* to the positive form. They form their superlative degree by adding *-st* or *-est* to the positive form.

Examples:

Positive	Comparative	Superlative
old	older	oldest
young	young	youngest
large	larger	largest

Adjectives of two or more syllables usually form their comparative and superlative degrees by adding *more* and *most.*

Examples:

beautiful	more beautiful	most beautiful
diligent	more diligent	most diligent
helpful	more helpful	most helpful

If you want to show decreased degrees of comparison, use the words *less* and *least.*

Examples:

Praying is *more* beneficial than gossiping.
Gossiping is *less* beneficial than praying.

Some adjectives are compared in an irregular manner.

Examples:

bad	worse	worst
good	better	best
little	less	least

Some adjectives can not be compared because they are absolute terms.

Examples:

dead	full	unique
single	square	

NOTE: Avoid *double comparisons.*

Examples: Today is colder than yesterday. (Correct)
Today is *more colder* than yesterday. (Incorrect) *More* and the suffix — *er* are both comparative forms. Only *one* form is needed.

EXERCISE 4

Name the three degrees of comparison for adjectives.

1.
2.
3.

EXERCISE 5

In the space at the right, tell what degree of comparison is used in the underlined word.

1. My fruit is *better* than gold, yea, than fine gold. Proverbs 8:19 ____________
2. He that gathers in summer is a *wise* man. Proverbs 9:5 ____________
3. Reading the Bible every day is the *best* way to gain understanding. ____________

EXERCISE 6

Circle the correct form of the adjective in the following sentences:

1. For most people the book of Ezekiel is the (most difficultest story, most difficult of all of the stories) in the Bible.
2. The story of Ezekiel is (most unique, unique).
3. Ezekiel claims the (highest, most high) degree of inspiration.
4. The words "Thus saith Jehovah" are repeated (more, most) often than the words, "I said."
5. Of the three books on prophecy— Daniel, Revelation, and Ezekiel, the book of Ezekiel contains the (more, most) mysterious imagery for me.
6. Of all the students in our class, my friend read the book (quicker, quickest).
7. My friend read the book (quicker, quickest) than I.

CHAPTER 13

MORE LEARNING ABOUT ADVERBS

In Chapter 5 you learned that adverbs are words which expand the meanings of verbs, adjectives, and other adverbs.

Adverbs, like adjectives, can also show degrees of comparison.

LESSON 13-A LEARNING ABOUT DEGREES OF COMPARISON

- The degrees of comparison are the *positive*, the *comparative*, and the *superlative*.

Examples:

a. Positive — used to show the existence of a situation.
— Read your *Bible frequently.* (*Frequently* is the adverb telling how often.)

b. Comparative — used in comparing two situations.
— Read your *Bible more frequently* than your devotional book. (*More frequently* is the comparative form of the adverb.)

c. Superlative — used in comparing more than two situations.
— Read your *Bible* the *most frequently* of all other books. (Most frequently is the superlative form of the adverb.)

The suffixes *-er* and *-est* may be added to the adverbs to form the comparisons. However, most adverbs form their degrees of comparison by adding the words *more, most, less,* and *least* before the adverb.

Examples:

carefully	more carefully	most carefully

Some adverbs can not be compared. Words like *not, very, almost,* and *only* do not change their form.

Some adverbs have irregular forms for the comparative and superlative degrees.

Examples:

a.	well	better	best
b.	badly	worse	worst
c.	far	farther	farthest (distance)
d.	far	further	furthest (quantity)

LESSON 13-B LEARNING TO AVOID ERRORS IN THE USE OF ADJECTIVES AND ADVERBS

In speaking English or in writing English, many people make errors in the use of adjectives and adverbs. Be careful about the following problems.

1. Avoid double comparisons: Do not use *-er* or *-est* suffixes in addition to the words *more, most, less,* and *least.*

   Example:

   (Incorrect) a. There is something *more better* than to eat and drink and enjoy life.

   (Correct) b. There is something *better* than to eat and drink and enjoy life.

   The *comparative* form uses either *-er* or *more,* not both.

2. Avoid using the comparative or superlative forms of adjectives and adverbs which can not be compared.

   Example:

   (Incorrect) a. Ecclesiastes paints a *most perfect* picture of the worldly man.

   (Correct) b. Ecclesiastes paints a *perfect* picture of the worldly man.

   Some qualities can not be compared, such as *unique, full, perfect.* Standards for these words are changing, however. Watch and listen for their usage in newspapers, books, and lectures.

3. Avoid making comparisons which are illogical or not clear.

   Example:

   (Incorrect) a. Solomon, the writer of Ecclesiastes, was *wiser* than any king in the Bible.

   (Correct) b. Solomon, the writer of Ecclesiastes, was *wiser than any other* king in the Bible.

   When comparing members of a group, use *else* or *other* with the comparative and *all* with the superlative.

4. Avoid using an adverb when an adjective is needed.

   Example:

   (Incorrect) a. Solomon felt *sadly* about the disillusionment of life.

   (Correct) b. Solomon felt *sad* about the disillusionment of life.

   Remember that predicate adjectives follow linking verbs. On the other hand, if the linking verb indicates action, then the adverbial form is needed.

5. Avoid using adjectives when an adverb is needed.

Example:

(Incorrect) a. The king was *real happy* when he found the truth of life.

(Correct) b. The king was *really happy* when he found the truth of life.

Adjectives modify nouns; adverbs modify adjectives. Therefore, the adverb *really* is needed to modify the adjective *happy.*

Other adjectives which cause problems are *good, sure,* and *most.* The adverbial forms are *well, surely,* and *almost.* When using these words, make certain that the correct word is applied.

EXERCISE 1

Select the correct word or phrase in the parenthesis in the following sentences.

1. A stone is heavy and the sand mighty, but a fool's wrath is (more heavier, heavier) than them both. (Proverbs 27:3)
2. Methuselah lived longer than (anyone, anyone else) in the Bible. (Genesis 5:27)
3. Don't feel (bad, badly) if you don't understand everything that you read for the first time.
4. The meal tasted (delicious, deliciously).
5. (Most, Almost) every person in America has heard the Gospel at least once.
6. They will (sure, surely) be held accountable to God.
7. Some say they can not preach (good, well).
8. Everyone is able to give a (real, really) good testimony of his salvation.
9. After a little practice, you will do (well, good).
10. (Sure, surely) men ought always to pray. (I Thessalonians 5:17)

EXPLORING TRUTHS

Let God speak to you through His Word. Look up the following verses. Concentrate on the adverbs *always, also,* and *once.* Then write what these adverbs mean to you.

Genesis 6:3

Deuteronomy 14:23

Psalm 16:8

Matthew 28:20

Philippians 4:4

Romans 6:10

Hebrews 9:27

I Peter 3:18

TEST ON ADJECTIVES AND ADVERBS

I. Adjectives modify ______ and ________.

II. Adverbs modify ______, __________ and ________.

III. The three degrees of comparison are the __________, the __________, and the __________.

IV. When comparing two qualities or situations, use the _______ degree.

V. When comparing more than two qualities or situations, use the __________ degree.

VI. Write the comparative and superlative of the following:

1. well ________________ ________________
2. tall ________________ ________________
3. easy ________________ ________________
4. good ________________ ________________
5. recent ________________ ________________

VII. Choose the correct word or phrase in the parenthesis in the following sentences.

1. The book of Esther is a (real, really) thrilling story of God's Providence in our lives.
2. (Most, Almost) all Jews were to be killed.
3. Esther (sure, surely) worked carefully to save the Jews.
4. Her foster father, Mordecai, was (smarter, more smarter) than Haman.
5. Haman's trickery was one of the (most clever, most clever of all) in the Bible.
6. Esther was (prettier than anyone in the realm, prettier than anyone else in the realm).
7. The Feast of Purim is (most always, almost always) celebrated by Jewish people.
8. The king felt very (bad, badly) about his decision to kill Mordecai.
9. The gallows designed by Haman was (dreadful, most dreadful).
10. God (sure, surely) does look after his own.

CHAPTER 14

MORE LEARNING ABOUT PREPOSITIONS

In Chapter 6 you learned about prepositions and prepositional phrases.

- A *prepositional phrase* is a group of words without a subject or predicate which acts as one part of speech in the sentence. Prepositional phrases can be used as adjectives or adverbs.

LESSON 14-A LEARNING ABOUT PREPOSITIONAL PHRASES USED AS ADJECTIVES

- When the prepositional phrase describes or modifies a noun or pronoun, the phrase is a prepositional phrase used as an adjective.

Example:

Paul talked about the sufferings *of Christ.* (The prepositional phrase *of Christ* describes the noun *sufferings.*)

EXERCISE 1

All of the prepositional phrases which are underlined in the following sentences are used as adjectives. In the space at the right, tell what word the phrase modifies.

1. All the promises *of God* are yea and amen. II Corinthians 1:20 ____________
2. For we know that if our earthly house *of this tabernacle* were dissolved, ____________
3. We have a building *of God.* II Corinthians 5:1 ____________
4. Where the Spirit *of the Lord* is, there is liberty. II Corinthians 3:17 ____________
5. God has made us able ministers *of the new testament.* II Corinthians 3:6 ____________

LESSON 14-B LEARNING ABOUT PREPOSITIONAL PHRASES USED AS ADVERBS

- When the prepositional phrase modifies a verb, adverb, or adjective, and when the phrase answers the questions *how, when,* or *where,* the phrase is used as an *adverb.*

Examples:

a. Jesus walked *with haste.* (How?)
b. Jesus walked *in the evening.* (When?)
c. Jesus walked *along the Sea of Galilee.* (Where?)

EXERCISE 2

All of the prepositional phrases which are underlined in the following sentences are used as adverbs. In the space at the right, tell what word the phrase modifies.

1. For with the heart man believeth *unto righteousness.* ________
2. And with the mouth confession is made *unto salvation.* ________
3. For whosoever shall call *upon the name* of the Lord shall be saved. ________
4. How then shall they call *on him* in whom they have not believed? ________
5. And how shall they believe *in him* of whom they have not heard? ________
6. And how shall they hear *without a preacher?* ________

from Romans 10:10-14

EXERCISE 3

Now tell whether the underlined phrases are *adjective phrases* or *adverb phrases.*

1. I beseech you, therefore, brethren, (a) *by the mercies* (b) *of God* that ye present your bodies a living sacrifice, holy, acceptable (c) *unto God,* which is your reasonable service.

a. ________
b. ________
c. ________

2. And be not conformed (d) *to this world* but be ye transformed (e) *by the renewing* (f) *of your mind,* that ye may prove what is that good and acceptable and perfect will (g) *of God.*

d. ________
e. ________
f. ________
g. ________

LESSON 14-C LEARNING TO AVOID ERRORS IN THE USE OF PREPOSITIONS

1. Avoid using the preposition *of* as a verb.

   Example:

   Moses might *of* been allowed to enter the promised land if he had controlled his temper. (*Of* is used as a verb. *Have* should have been used in place of the word *of.*)

2. Be careful about the use of *beside* and *besides. Beside* means by the side of; *besides* means in addition to.

   Example:

   Besides Miriam and Aaron, many Israelites walked *beside* Moses.

3. Avoid using prepositions that are not necessary.

   Example:

   a. Where is the book at? (At is not necessary to complete the meaning of the sentence.)

   b. Do not jump off *of* the bridge. (*Of* is unnecessary.)

4. Be careful about the use of *between* and *among*. The two words have the same meaning, but *between* is used when showing a relationship between two nouns. *Among* is used to show a relationship between more than two nouns.

   Example:

   a. May the Lord watch *between* you and me.
   Genesis 31:49

   b. And I will dwell *among* the children of Israel and will be their God. Genesis 29:45

5. Be careful to place the prepositional phrases near the words which are modified. Otherwise, a ridiculous sentence occurs.

   Example:

   (Incorrect) Judah and his brothers fell before Joseph on the ground. (Who was on the ground? Joseph or his brothers?)

   (Correct) Judah and his brothers fell on the ground before Joseph.

TEST ON CHAPTER 14

I. Circle the correct forms in the following sentences.

1. Paul (could of been, could have been) the writer of Hebrews.
2. There were other authors of the books in the New Testament (besides, beside) Paul.
3. Where was (Paul, Paul at) when he was blinded by a light from heaven?
4. (Between you and me, Between you and I), I (would have been, would of been) frightened.
5. (Between Paul and Timothy, Among Paul and Timothy) there was a great love.

II. Underline the prepositional phrases in the following sentences. In the space at the right, tell whether the phrases are adjective phrases or adverb phrases.

1. Therefore being justified by faith, we have peace with God through our Lord Jesus Christ.
2. By whom also we have access by faith into this grace wherein we stand and rejoice in hope of the glory of God.
3. But God commendeth His love toward us, in that, while we were yet sinners, Christ died for us.

a. ____________
b. ____________
c. ____________
d. ____________
e. ____________
f. ____________
g. ____________
h. ____________
i. ____________
j. ____________
k. ____________

Chapter 15

MORE LEARNING ABOUT CONJUNCTIONS

In Chapter 7 the three kinds of conjunctions were discussed. Sometimes, in formal English, confusion exists over the use of certain conjunctions.

LESSON 15-A LEARNING TO USE APPROPRIATE EXPRESSIONS

There are several sets of words that are used informally which are not acceptable in formal English.

1. like — as.

   Like is a preposition. *As* and *as if* are subordinating conjunctions.

   Examples:

   a. Walk *like* the son of a king.
   b. Walk *as if* you were the son of a king.

2. etc.

   Means *and so forth.* Therefore, do not use the word *and* before *etc.*

   Examples:

   On your vacation be certain to swim, bike, play ball, etc.

3. Avoid using *where* for *that* or *which.*

   Example:

   It tells in Genesis 39 *that* (not where) Joseph found favor with the Lord.

4. different from — different than.

   Different from is used when a prepositional phrase follows. *Different than* is used when a clause follows.

   Examples:

   a. Joseph's robe was different from mine.
   b. Joseph's robe was different than that worn by his brother.

5. because — on account of.

   The preposition is *on account of.* The subordinating conjunction is *because.*

   Examples:

   a. Joseph was thrown into prison on account of the queen's sin.
   b. Joseph was thrown into prison because the queen had sinned.

6. Avoid using *and* too many times in one sentence.

Example:

(Poor Sentence Structure)	Joseph was put into prison and the guards bound him and Joseph behaved himself and the guards became kind to him.
(Improved)	Joseph was put into prison. There the guards bound him. Because he behaved himself, the guards became kind to him.

7. Avoid using *and* and *so* as transitional words.

Example:

(Poor Sentence Structure)	The butler and the baker offended the king. So Pharaoh was wroth. And he put them in prison, too.
(Improved)	The butler and the baker offended the king. Pharaoh was wroth. Therefore, he put them in prison, too.

EXPLORING TRUTHS

Conjunctions seem unimportant to our langauge other than to combine thoughts. Look up the following references and see how exciting a little word can be.

Acts 6:7	What outstanding event occurred because of certain conditions? Notice that the word *and* calls this event to our attention.
Acts 12:24	What conjunction is used? What happened?
Acts 19:20	What conjunction is used here? What followed?

Be aware of conjunctions and their value in understanding Scripture.

What books in the Old Testament begin with *"And"*? What does this tell you about their place in the canon of Scripture?

TEST ON CHAPTER 15

Please review Chapter 7 before using this test.

I. Name 5 coordinating conjunctions.

1.
2.
3.
4.
5.

II. Name 3 sets of correlative conjunctions.

1.
2.
3.

III. Circle the correct form in the following sentences.

1. Paul's style of writing is (different from, different that) Luke's.
2. Luke wrote (like, as) a professional author.
3. The Acts of the Apostles is the book (where, in which) Luke writes about exciting events in believers' lives.
4. (Because, On account of) the storm, Paul warned the sailors to be calm.
5. The Gospel of Luke describes the background of John the Baptist, the birth of Jesus, the temptations of Jesus, the parables of Jesus, (and etc., etc.).

TEST ON PART TWO

I. In the space at the right, tell how each underlined noun is used. Choose from the words subject, predicate noun, direct object, indirect object, object of preposition, noun of direct address, possessive noun, appositive, objective complement, or retained object. The first one has been done.

1. The *Lord* (a) is in his holy *temple;* (b) the *Lord's* (c) throne is in heaven: his *eyes* (d) behold, his eyelids try the *children* (e) of men. (Psalm 11:4)

a. subject
b. ____
c. ____
d. ____
e. ____

2. God will show the *believer* (f) the path of life; in his presence is *fullness* (g) of joy. (Psalm 16:11)

f. ____
g. ____

3. God is our *refuge* (h) and *strength,* (i) a very present *help* (j) in trouble. (Psalm 46:1)

h. ____
i. ____
j. ____

4. The angel said, "Fear not, *Mary,* (k) for thou shall bring forth a son and shall call his name *Jesus."* (l) (Luke 1:31)

k. ____
l. ____

II. In the spaces at the right, tell how each underlined pronoun is used. Is it a subject, direct object, etc.?

1. Ask of *me* (a) and I shall give *you* (b) the heathen for *thine (your)* (c) inheritance. (Psalm 2:8)

a. ____
b. ____
c. ____

2. I laid *me* (d) down and slept. *I* (e) awaked; for the Lord sustained *me.* (f) (Psalm 3:5)

d. ____
e. ____
f. ____

3. Christians, it is *we* (g) who should tell the world about Jesus.

g. ____

III. Circle the correct verb in the following sentences.

1. But know that the Lord has (sit, set) apart him that is godly for himself. (Psalm 4:3)
2. The Lord is (known, knowed) by the judgment which he executeth. (Psalm 9:16)

3. The Lord looked down from heaven upon the children of men to see if there (was, were) any that did understand and seek God. (Psalm 14:2)
4. They are all (gone, went) aside; they are all together become filthy. (Psalm 14:3)
5. Some (trusts, trust) in chariots and some in horses; but we (shall, will) remember the name of the Lord our God. (Psalm 20:7)
6. They are (brung, brought) down and (felled, fallen); but we are (raised, risen) and stand upright. (Psalm 20:8)

IV. Decide whether the verbs in the following sentences are in the active voice or the passive voice.

1. *Mark* (a) the perfect man and *behold* (b) the upright for the end of that man is peace. (Psalm 37:37)
   a. ________
   b. ________
2. But the transgressors *shall be destroyed* (c) together.
   c. ________
3. The end of the wicked *shall be cut off.* (d) (Psalm 37:37)
   d. ________

V. Circle the predicate adjectives in the following sentences.

1. I am weary with my groaning. (Psalm 6:6)
2. What is man that thou art mindful of him? (Psalm 8:4)
3. God is angry with the wicked every day. (Psalm 7:11)
4. The law of the Lord is perfect, converting the soul; the testimony of the Lord is sure, making wise the simple.
5. The statutes of the Lord are right, rejoicing the heart; the commandment of the Lord is pure, enlightening the eyes. (Psalm 19:7 and 8)

VI. Write the three degrees of comparison for the following words.

	Positive	Comparative	Superlative
1.	lovely	________	________
2.	________	less	________
3.	________	________	most
4.	circular	________	________

PART III

VERBALS

LEARNING ABOUT VERBALS

In chapter 6 you learned that a phrase is a group of words without a subject and predicate which is used as a single part of speech. You have studied verb phrases and prepositional phrases. Now learn about verbals.

The *verbal phrases* are as follows:

- **THE PARTICIPIAL PHRASE**
- **THE GERUND PHRASE**
- **THE INFINITIVE PHRASE**

They are called verbal phrases because the most important word in them is a verbal. Verbals are so called because they are formed from verbs. In some respects they act like verbs. For instance, they may express action; they may be modified by adverbs; and they may take objects. In one important respect, however, they are not like verbs. Verbals are not used as verbs in a sentence. They are used as other parts of speech: as nouns, as adjectives, and as adverbs.

EXERCISE 1

Name the three kinds of verbals.

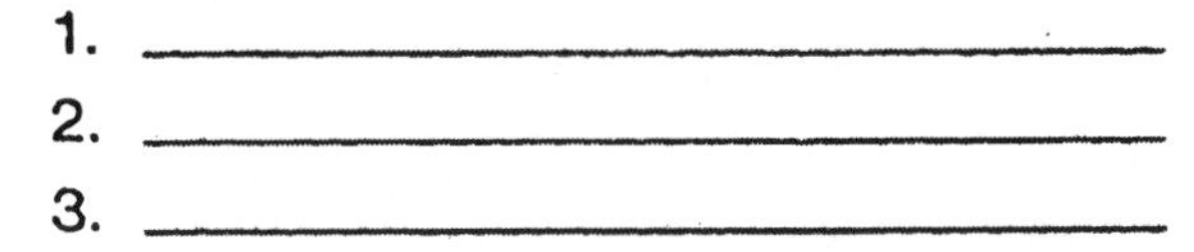

1. ______________________________
2. ______________________________
3. ______________________________

CHAPTER 16

LEARNING ABOUT PARTICIPLES

LESSON 16-A RECOGNITION OF PARTICIPLES

• A *participle* is a verb form used as an adjective.

Like verbs, participles have different forms to show tense and voice.

The *present participle* is formed by adding the suffix *-ing* to the present tense of the verb.

Examples:

a. The Lord shall cut off all *flattering* lips. (Psalm 12:3)

b. The wicked sit in the *lurking* places of the village.

The *past* or *perfect participle* is the fourth principal part of the verb and ends in *-ed, -d, -t, -en* or *-n,* except in irregular verbs. See pp. 91 and 92.

Example:

Remember all the offerings and accept thy *burnt* sacrifice.
(Psalm 20:3).

• Sometimes a participle follows a linking verb and modifies the subject. The participle then takes the pattern of a predicate adjective.

Example:

He is *despised* and *rejected* of men. (Isaiah 53:3)
(*Despised* and *rejected* are participles. Some grammarians call *is despised* a verb phrase. However, when the predicate adjective can be compared, it is not a verb phrase, but a participle.)

EXERCISE 2

Underline the participles in the following sentences. In the blank at the right, tell what noun or pronoun the participles modifies.

1. We did esteem him stricken, smitten of God, and afflicted. (Isaiah 53:4) __________
2. He was oppressed, and he was afflicted, yet he opened not his mouth. (Isaiah 53:7) __________
3. But let patience have her perfect work, that you may be perfect and entire wanting nothing. (James 1:4) __________
4. He [the righteous] shall not be afraid of evil things: his heart is fixed, trusting in the Lord. (Psalm 112:7) __________
5. The law of the Lord is perfect, converting the soul: __________ the testimony of the Lord is sure, making wise the simple. (Psalm 19:7)

• Both the *present* and the *past participle* may be used as a verb or as part of a verb phrase. When the participle is used as an adjective, it becomes a verbal.

Examples:

a. The lion *was roaring* in the cage. (*Roaring* is used as a part of the verb phrase, was roaring.)

b. They gaped at me as a *roaring* lion. (*Roaring* is used as an adjective and is a present participle.)

LESSON 16-B RECOGNITION OF PARTICIPIAL PHRASES

• The participle may be used alone as in some of the above examples, or it may have modifiers and objects. The participle with its modifiers is called a *participial phrase.*

Example:

The righteous shall be like a tree *planted by the rivers of water.*

EXERCISE 3

Underline the participles in the following sentences. Place parentheses around the participial phrases. In the space at the right, write the noun which the participle or the participial phrase modifies.

Example:

The *fear* of the Lord is clean, (enduring forever). fear

1. The commandment of the Lord is pure, enlightening the eyes. (Psalm 19:8b) ________
2. The Lord will hear his anointed from his holy heaven with the saving strength of his right hand. (Psalm 20:6) ________
3. And many of the brethren in the Lord, waxing confident by my bonds, are much more bold to speak the word without fear. (Phil. 1:14) ________
4. The one preach Christ of contention, not sincerely, supposing to add affliction to my bonds: (Phil. 1:16) ________
5. But the other of love, knowing that I am set for the defense of the Gospel. (Phil. 1:17) ________
6. For I am in a strait betwixt two, having a desire to depart, and to be with Christ; which is far better: (Phil. 1:23) ________
7. And having this confidence, I know that I shall abide and continue with you all for your furtherance and joy of faith; (Phil. 1:25) ________
8. Because for the work of Christ he was nigh unto death, not regarding his life, to supply your lack of service toward me. (Phil. 2:30) ________

9. That ye might walk worthy of the Lord unto all pleasing, being fruitful in every good work, and increasing in the knowledge of God; (Col. 1:10) ________
10. Strengthened with all might, according to his glorious power, unto all patience and longsuffering with joyfulness; (Col. 1:11) ________
11. Giving thanks unto the Father, which hath made us meet to be partakers of the inheritance of the saints in light: (Col. 1:12) ________

LESSON 16-C CONJUGATION OF PARTICIPLES

Tense	Active Voice	Passive Voice
Present	planting	being planted
Past		planted
Perfect	having planted	having been planted
Perfect Progressive	having been planting	

LESSON 16-D DANGLING PARTICIPLES

The participle is known as a *dangler* when it is not related to a noun or pronoun in the sentence.

Example:

(Incorrect) a. Singing in the choir, a loud noise interrupted the song. (*Singing* in the choir seems to modify noise.)

(Correct) b. The soloist, singing in the choir, was interrupted by a loud noise. (*Singing* in the choir modifies soloist.)

LESSON 16-E PUNCTUATION OF PARTICIPIAL PHRASES

You have learned that a participle is a verb form used as an adjective. The participle may have objects, modifiers and complements and become a participial phrase.

- When the participial phrase identifies a noun or a pronoun, no comma is needed. A *restrictive phrase* is the name given to these phrases.

Example:

Then was brought unto him one *possessed with a devil.*
(Matt. 12:22)

• When the participial phrase supplies additional information, it is called a *nonrestrictive phrase* which should be separated from the rest of the sentence by commas.

Example:

When an unclean spirit is gone out of a man, he walks through dry places, *seeking rest,* and finds none. (Matt. 12:43)

• Introductory participial phrases are usually followed by a comma.

Example:

Desiring to speak with him, his mother and brothers stood without.

CHAPTER 17

LEARNING ABOUT GERUNDS

LESSON 17-A RECOGNITION OF GERUNDS

● A *gerund* is a verb form used as a noun. Like verbs and participles, the gerund has different forms to show tense and voice.

Gerunds are formed by adding *-ing* to the present tense of the verb.

Examples:

a. If you endure *chastening,* God deals with you as with sons. (Hebrews 12:7)

b. Man's *goings* are of the Lord. (Proverbs 20:24)

LESSON 17-B CONJUGATION OF GERUNDS

Tense	Active Voice	Passive Voice
Present	chastening	being chastened
Perfect	having chastened	having been chastened

LESSON 17-C USES OF GERUNDS

A gerund can be used as a subject, direct object, predicate nominative, appositive, or object of a preposition. A gerund may take objects or have modifiers.

Examples:

a. Subject–*Weeping* may endure for a night, but joy comes in the morning. (Psalm 30:5)

b. Direct Object–God understands our *weeping.*

c. Predicate nominative– Crying over lost souls is *weeping* before God.

d. Appositive–In Rama was there a voice heard, lamentation and *weeping,* (Matthew 2:18a)

e. Object of a preposition–So the days of *weeping* and mourning for Moses were ended. (Numbers 34:8)

LESSON 17-D RECOGNITION OF GERUND PHRASES

The gerund may be used alone or it may have modifiers and objects. The gerund with its modifiers is called a *gerund phrase.*

EXERCISE 1

Underline the gerunds in the following sentences. Place parentheses around the gerund phrase. In the space at the right, tell how the gerund is used.

Example:

There was (great mourning among the Jews, and fasting and weeping, and wailing.) ___subject___

1. Jehoiada appointed the offices of the house of the Lord to offer the burnt offerings with rejoicing and with singing. (II Chronicles 23:18) ________ ________
2. And it came to pass, as the trumpeters and singers were as one, to make one sound to be heard in praising and thanking the Lord. (II Chronicles 5:3) ________ ________
3. And the Lord hath blessed thee since my coming. (Genesis 30:30) ________
4. And when Eli heard the noise of the crying, he said, "What meaneth the noise of this tumult?" (I Samuel 4:14) ________
5. He saith among the trumpets, Ha, Ha; and he smelleth the battle afar off, the thunder of the captains, and the shouting. (Job 39:25) ________
6. And when she had done giving him drink, she said, I will draw *water* for the camels also, until they have done drinking. (Genesis 24:19) ________ ________

EXERCISE 2

In the blank at the right, tell whether the underlined word is a verb, gerund or a participle.

1. When it goeth well with the righteous, the city rejoiceth; and when the wicked perish, there is shouting. (Proverbs 11:10) ________
2. Serve the Lord with gladness, come before his presence with singing. (Psalm 100:2) ________
3. I will sing of mercy and judgment. (Psalm 101:1) ________
4. The singing heart pleases God. ________
5. And the shepherds returned, glorifying and praising God for all the things that they had heard and seen. (Luke 2:20) ________ ________
6. And they sang together by course in praising and giving thanks unto the Lord. (Ezra 3:11) ________
7. Blessed are they that dwell in thy house; they will be still praising thee. (Psalm 84:4) ________ ________

CHAPTER 18

LEARNING ABOUT INFINITIVES

LESSON 18-A RECOGNITION OF INFINITIVES

• The *infinitive* is a verb form used as an adjective, an adverb, or a noun. It is usually formed by adding *to* plus the present tense of a verb.

Examples:

a. to pray, to clap
b. Have you a desire *to obey* God? (*To obey* is an infinitive used as an adjective modifying desire.)
c. We read the Bible *to learn* about God. (*To learn* is an infinitive used as an adverb.)
d. *To obey* is better than sacrifice. (*To obey* is an infinitive used as a subject of the sentence.)
e. Our aim should be *to obey* God. (*To obey* is an infinitive used as a predicate nominative.)
f. We desire *to obey* God. (*To obey* is used as direct object of the verb desire.)

LESSON 18-B CONJUGATION OF INFINITIVES

Like verbs, participles, and gerunds, infinitives have different forms to show tense and voice.

Tense	Active Voice	Passive Voice
Present	to pray	to be prayed
Present Progressive	to be praying	
Perfect	to have prayed	to have been prayed
Perfect Progressive	to have been praying	

NOTE: Be careful to recognize the difference between a prepositional phrase and an infinitive phrase.

Example:

a. to them—*to* is a preposition followed by the pronoun *them*.
b. to go—*to* plus the verb *go* is an infinitive.

LESSON 18-C RECOGNITION OF INFINITIVE PHRASES

• Like other verbals, the infinitives with its modifiers is called an *infinitive phrase.*

Example:

In the following sentence, the infinitive phrases are placed in parentheses and the infinitive is underlined.

I know both how (<u>to be abased</u>), and I know how (<u>to abound</u> everywhere) and in all things I am instructed both (<u>to be</u> full) and (<u>to be</u> hungry) both (<u>to abound</u>) and (<u>to suffer</u>). (Philippians 4:12)

EXERCISE 1

Underline the infinitives in the following sentences. Place parentheses around the infinitive phrases.

1. Whereof I am made a minister, according to the dispensation of God which is given to me for you, to fulfill the Word of God. (Colosslans 1:25)
2. As I besought thee to abide still at Ephesus, when I went into Macedonia, that you might charge some that they teach no other doctrine. (I Timothy 1:15)
3. This is a faithful saying and worthy of all acceptation, that Christ Jesus came into the world to save sinners; of whom I am chief. (I Timothy 1:15)
4. Of whom is Hymenaeus and Alexander; whom I have delivered unto Satan, that they may learn not to blaspheme. (I Timothy 1:20)
5. God will have all men to be saved, and to come into the knowledge of the truth. (I Timothy 2:4)
6. God gave himself a ransom for all, to be testified in due time. (I Timothy 2:6)
7. But I suffer not a woman to teach, nor to usurp authority over the man, but to be in silence. (I Timothy 2:12)

NOTE: Sometimes an infinitive appears without the word *to*. This happens after such verbs as dare, help, let, make, need, and order.

Example:

Let another man *praise* thee. (Proverbs 27:2)

LESSON 18-D SPLIT INFINITIVES

- The *split infinitive* occurs when *to* is separated from the verb.

Some grammar books state the rule: Never split an infinitive. Most formal writers of English avoid the split infinitive. Some authorities state: Do not split an infinitive except for emphasis.

Study the following sentences.

1. I want to immediately pray. (Unnecessary split)
2. I want to pray immediately.
3. I want to really pray immediately. (Emphasis)

LESSON 18-E THE USE OF PRONOUNS WITH INFINITIVES, GERUNDS, AND PARTICIPLES

- Sometimes difficulty occurs in selecting the correct pronouns for the *subject* of an infinitive. The subject of an infinitive is always in the objective case.

Example:

So David stayed his servants with these words, and suffered *them* not to rise against Saul. (The infinitive phrase is *them not to rise against Saul. Them* is the subject of the infinitive *to rise.*)

EXERCISE 2

Place parentheses around the infinitive phrase and underline the subject of the infinitive. See the example above.

1. It is vain for you to rise up early, to sit up late, to eat the bread of sorrows. (Psalm 127:2)
2. Behold, how good and how pleasant it is for brethren to dwell together in unity. (Psalm 133:1)
3. Do good, O Lord, unto those that be good, and to them that are upright in their hearts. (Psalm 125:4)
4. And let them have dominion over the fish of the sea. (Genesis 1:26b)
5. Now set your heart and your soul to seek the Lord your God. (I Chronicles 22:19)

LESSON 18-F

• Problems also arise in selecting the correct pronouns for the predicate nominative following an infinitive.

Example:

God elected Jesus to be Him who would die for the sins of the world.

Notice that the pronoun *him* must be objective because the noun to which it refers is Jesus, the direct object of the verb elected.

Remember: The same case after *to be* as before *to be.*

LESSON 18-G USING PRONOUNS

• The case of the pronoun used in front of a gerund or a participle is determined by the emphasis desired.

Examples:

a. I enjoy *his* singing. (The possessive case of pronouns usually precedes a gerund. Here the emphasis is on the act of singing.)
b. I enjoyed him singing. (The emphasis is on the person rather than on the act of singing.)

EXPLORING TRUTHS

Paul's letters abound with verbal expressions. Read Ephesians 5. Make a list of all of the participles in the chapter. To whom are these participles referring? If you want a radiant Christian life, apply the participial phrases to your life.

TEST ON VERBALS

I. The three kinds of verbals are:

1.
2.
3.

II. Fill in the blanks in the following sentences.

1. An infinitive is a __________ form that begins with the word __________ and is used as either a __________, an __________ or an __________.
2. A participle is a __________ form used as an __________.
3. A gerund is a __________ form ending in __________ that is always used in a sentence as a __________.

III. Enclose all the verbal phrases in the following sentences with parentheses. In the blanks at the right identify the kind of verbal.

A. But without faith it is impossible to please him: for he that cometh to God must believe that he is, and that he is a rewarder of them that diligently seek him. (Hebrews 11:6)

a. ________

B. By faith Noah, being warned of God of things not seen as yet, moved with fear, prepared an ark to the saving of his house; (Hebrews 11:7a)

b. ________
c. ________
d. ________

C. These all died in faith, not having received the promises, but having seen them afar off, and were persuaded of them, and embraced them, and confessed that they were strangers and pilgrims on the earth. (Hebrews 11:13)

e. ________
f. ________

D. By faith Moses, when he was come to years, refused to be called the son of Pharaoh's daughter; choosing rather to suffer affliction with the people of God, than to enjoy the pleasures of sin for a season; (Hebrews 11:24 & 25)

g. ________
h. ________
i. ________

E. Now no chastening for the present seemeth to be joyous, but grievous: nevertheless afterward it yieldeth the peaceable fruit of righteousness unto them which are exercised thereby. (Hebrews 12:11)

j. ________
k. ________

PART IV

SENTENCE STRUCTURE

- A *sentence* is a single word or a group of words that expresses a single purpose. In most cases, a sentence has a subject and a verb. In an elliptical sentence, only a piece of a sentence is given.

CHAPTER 19

LEARNING ABOUT SIMPLE SENTENCES

LESSON 19-A RECOGNITION OF A SIMPLE SENTENCE

There are five kinds of *simple sentences:*

- *Declarative* sentence—a sentence that makes a statement. Punctuate a declarative sentence with a period.

  Examples:

  a. And Jesus went out and departed from the temple. (Matthew 24:1a)

  b. His disciples came to him for to show him the building of the temple. (Matthew 24:1b)

- *Interrogative* sentence—a sentence which asks a question. Punctuate an interrogative sentence with a question mark.

  Examples:

  a. And Jesus said unto them, "Do you not see all things?" (Matthew 24:2a)

  b. The disciples asked, "When shall these things be?" (Matthew 24:3)

- *Imperative* sentence—a sentence which expresses a command or a request. Punctuate an imperative with a period.

  Examples:

  a. Take heed that no man deceive you. (Matthew 24:4)

  b. Endure until the end, and be saved. (Matthew 24:13)

- *Exclamatory* sentence—a sentence that expresses strong feeling. Punctuate an exclamatory sentence with an exclamation point.

  Examples:

  a. Then shall be great tribulation! (Matthew 24:21)

  b. For as the lightening cometh out of the East, and shineth unto the West, so shall also the coming of the Son of man be! (Matthew 24:27)

- *Elliptical* sentence—a piece of a sentence or a group of words that expresses a thought. Punctuate an elliptical sentence according to the meaning expressed.

  Examples:

  a. The end times? or The end times.

  b. What hour?

EXERCISE 1

In the space at the right, indicate the kind of sentence which it is. Punctuate the sentence correctly.

Remember that a simple sentence may contain a compound subject and/or a compound predicate.

1. Then Judas Iscariot went to the chief priests __ __________
2. He said, "What will you give me __" __________
3. They covenanted with him for 30 pieces of silver __ __________
4. Thirty pieces of silver __ __________
5. The disciples said to Jesus, "Where will we prepare the passover __" __________
6. Go to the city __ __________
7. Jesus sat with the twelve __ __________
8. One of you shall betray me __ __________
9. Lord, is it I __ __________
10. Woe unto that man by whom the Son of Man is betrayed __ __________

from Matthew 26:14-24

EXERCISE 2

Name the five kinds of simple sentences.

1.
2.
3.
4.
5.

CHAPTER 20

LEARNING ABOUT COMPOUND SENTENCES

LESSON 20-A RECOGNITION OF A COMPOUND SENTENCE

You have learned that a simple sentence is a group of words with a subject and a verb. The simple sentence begins with a capital letter and ends with a period, question mark, or exclamation point.

- When two simple sentences are joined together in certain patterns, a *compound sentence* is formed.

Examples:

a. One generation passes away, and another generation comes. (Two simple sentences are connected by the coordinating conjunction *and.* The comma suggests a pause.)

b. The wind goes toward the South; it whirls about continually. (Two simple sentences are joined together with a semicolon taking the place of a comma and a coordinating conjunction.)

c. All the rivers run into the sea; nevertheless, the sea is not full. (Here a semicolon is used, and the conjunctive adverb *nevertheless* becomes a connecting word.)

(Ecclesiastes 1:4, 6, 7)

LESSON 20-B LEARNING ABOUT CONJUNCTIVE ADVERBS

Conjunctive adverbs are used to connect two simple sentences. They also serve as adverbs. The most commonly used conjunctive adverbs are

- accordingly
- also
- besides
- consequently
- furthermore
- hence
- however
- indeed
- likewise
- nevertheless
- otherwise
- rather
- therefore
- thus

A semicolon is used before the conjunctive adverb in a compound sentence. A comma follows the conjunctive adverb. If the conjunctive adverb appears elsewhere in the sentence, it is set off by commas.

Examples:

a. The sleep of a laboring man is sweet; *however,* the abundance of the rich will not suffer him to sleep. (Ecclesiastes 5:12)

b. The sleep of a laboring man is sweet; the abundance of the rich, *however,* will not suffer him to sleep.

NOTE: A simple sentence may contain a compound subject or a compound verb. Therefore, be certain that punctuation marks are not used carelessly in simple sentences.

INCORRECT: The sun goes down, and hastens to his place.

CORRECT: The *sun goes* down and *hastens* to his place. (No comma is needed because this is a simple sentence with a compound verb.) (Ecclesiastes 1:5)

EXERCISE 1

Place punctuation marks in the sentences below. In the space at the right, tell whether the sentence is a simple sentence or a compound sentence. Remember that a simple sentence may contain a compound subject and/or a compound predicate.

1. All things are full of labor man cannot utter it. (Ecclesiastes 1:8) __________
2. I made me great works I builded me houses I planted me vineyards. (Ecclesiastes 2:4) __________
3. I made me gardens and orchards and planted trees in them of all kinds. (Ecclesiastes 2:5) __________
4. I got me servants and maidens and had servants born to my house. (Ecclesiastes 2:7) __________
5. The wise man's eyes are in his head however the fool walks in darkness. (Ecclesiastes 2:14) __________
6. For all man's days are sorrows and his travail is grief. (Ecclesiastes 2:14) __________
7. He has made every thing beautiful in his time and has set the world in their hearts. (Ecclesiastes 3:11) __________
8. Every man should eat and drink and enjoy the good of his labor. (Ecclesiastes 3:13) __________
9. All is vanity and vexation of spirit. __________
10. To every thing there is a season and there is a time to every purpose under the sun. (Ecclesiastes 3:1) __________

CHAPTER 21

LEARNING ABOUT COMPLEX SENTENCES

LESSON 21-A RECOGNITION OF A COMPLEX SENTENCE

• A *complex sentence* is a sentence which contains an independent clause and one or more dependent clauses. To write and recognize a complex sentence, you must understand what a clause is.

LESSON 21-B LEARNING ABOUT CLAUSES

• A *clause* is a group of related words that contains a subject and a predicate.

• A clause which expresses an independent thought is called an *independent* or *main* clause. Therefore, a simple sentence is an *independent clause.* A compound sentence is composed of two or more independent clauses.

• A clause which is not complete in meaning by itself is called a *dependent* or *subordinate clause*. There are three kinds of *subordinate* clauses: adverbial clauses, adjective clauses, and noun clauses.

LESSON 21-C LEARNING ABOUT ADVERBIAL CLAUSES

• An *adverbial clause* is a *subordinate* clause which has the characteristics of an adverb. It tells *how, where, why, in what manner,* and *when.*

Examples:

a. *Once* a woman having an alabaster box of very precious ointment came to Jesus. (Once is an adverb.)

b. *In Bethany* a woman having an alabaster box of very precious ointment came to Jesus. (*In Bethany* is a prepositional phrase used as an adverb.)

c. *When Jesus was in Bethany*, a woman having an alabaster box of very precious ointment came to him. (*When Jesus was in Bethany* is an adverbial clause used as an adverb.)

from Matthew 26:6-7

EXERCISE 1

In the space at the right, tell whether the underlined words are adverbs, prepositional phrases, or adverbial clauses.

1. When his disciples saw it, they had indignation. ____________
2. To what purpose is this waste? ____________
3. You always have the poor with you. ____________
4. Because she poured this ointment on my body, she did it for my burial. ____________
5. Wheresoever this Gospel shall be preached in the whole world, this story shall be told for a memorial to her. ____________

from Matthew 26:8-13

LESSON 21-D LEARNING ABOUT SUBORDINATE CONJUNCTIONS

● *Subordinate conjunctions* are words used to introduce adverbial clauses. There are many such words, but listed below are a few common *subordinate conjunctions.*

after	because	in order that	unless
although	before	since	until
as	even if	so that	when
as few as	how	than	where
as little as	if	that	while

EXERCISE 2

In the space provided write as many subordinate conjunctions as you can.

EXERCISE 3

Place parentheses around the adverbial clauses in the following sentences.

1. When the first day of the feast of unleavened bread arrived, the disciples came to Jesus.
2. The disciples did as Jesus had appointed them.
3. Then they made ready the passover.
4. Now when the even was come, he sat down with the twelve.
5. As they did eat, he told them that one of them would betray him.
6. Jesus told them that he would not drink of this fruit of the vine until that day when he would break it new with them in his Father's kingdom.
7. When they had sung an hymn, they went out to the mount of Olives. from Matthew 26:17-30

NOTE: Introductory adverbial clauses are always set off by a comma.

LESSON 21-E LEARNING ABOUT ADJECTIVE CLAUSES

● An *adjective clause* is a subordinate clause which has the characteristics of an adjective. It modifies nouns and pronouns.

● Adjective clauses are also called *relative* clauses.

Examples:

a. Then Jesus went to a place *called Gethsemane.* (*Called Gethsemane* is a participial phrase used as an adjective.)

b. Then Jesus went to a place *which was called Gethsemane.* (*Which was called Gethsemane* is an adjective clause modifying the noun place.)

LESSON 21-F LEARNING ABOUT RELATIVE PRONOUNS.

• *Relative pronouns* are words used to introduce an adjective clause. There are six relative pronouns:

who	whose	whom
which	that	what

EXERCISE 4

In the space provided write 6 relative pronouns.

EXERCISE 5

Place parentheses around the adjective clauses in the following sentences.

1. The disciples whom Jesus took with him to Gethsemane fell asleep.
2. Jesus, who wanted to obey God's will, was exceeding sorrowful.
3. Jesus asked God to let this cup, which was very bitter, pass from him.
4. Nevertheless he said, "Thy will be done."
5. Judas, who was one of the twelve, came to Jesus with a great multitude with swords and staves.
6. Now he that betrayed Jesus gave them a sign.
7. Behold, one of them which were with Jesus stretched out his hand and drew his sword.
8. Jesus said unto him, "Put up the sword, for all they that take the sword shall perish with the sword. from Matthew 26:40-52

NOTE: If the adjective clause is needed in the sentence to identify the noun or pronoun which it modifies, no comma is needed. The clause is called a *restrictive* clause. (See sentence #1 exercise 5 above.)

• An adjective clause that adds extra information to the sentence needs to be set off by commas. It is called a *nonrestrictive clause.* (See sentence #2 in exercise 5 above.)

LESSON 21-G LEARNING ABOUT RELATIVE ADVERBS

• Sometimes the adjective clause is introduced by *when* or *where.* If the clause introduced by these words modifies a noun or pronoun, *when* and *where* are called *relative adverbs.*

Examples:

a. Gethsemane was the garden *where* Jesus prayed.
b. It was a time *when* Jesus wanted his disciples to join him.

LESSON 21-H LEARNING ABOUT NOUN CLAUSES

- A *noun clause* is one which can be used in any way that a noun functions. It is introduced by relative pronouns or subordinate conjunctions.

Examples:

a. I know *that* thou favourest me. (Psalm 41:11)
   (*That thou favourest me* is a noun clause used as a direct object of the verb *know.*)

b. *I know God's favour.*
   (*Favour* is a noun used as a direct object.)

c. That thou favourest me is known to me.
   (*That thou favourest me* is a noun clause used as the subject.)

EXERCISE 6

Place parentheses around the noun clauses in the following sentences. In the spaces at the right tell whether the clause was used as a subject, direct object, subject complement, or appositive.

1. You know that after two days is the feast of the passover. (Matthew 26:2) ____________
2. Do you think that Jesus could not pray to his Father? (Matthew 26:53) ____________
3. The high priest said that Jesus had spoken blasphemy. (Matthew 26:53) ____________
4. That Jesus would ever speak blasphemy is an illogical statement. ____________
5. The truth is that Jesus spoke only what would please God. ____________

EXERCISE 7

Place parentheses around the subordinate clauses in the following sentences. In the spaces at the right tell whether the clause is an adverbial clause, an adjective clause, or a noun clause.

1. When the morning was come, all the chief priests and elders of the people took counsel against Jesus to put him to death. ____________
2. And when they had bound him, they led him away, and delivered him to Pontius Pilate the governor. ____________
3. Then Judas, which had betrayed him, when he saw that he was condemned, repented himself, and brought again the thirty pieces of silver to the chief priests and elders. ____________ ____________
4. Saying, I have sinned in that I have betrayed the innocent blood. ____________
5. And when he was accused of the chief priests and elders, he answered nothing. ____________
6. Now at that feast the governor was wont to release unto the people a prisoner, whom they would. ____________

7. For he knew that for envy they had delivered him. ___________
8. When he was set down on the judgment seat, his wife sent unto him, saying, "Have thou nothing to do with that just man." ___________

from Matthew 27:1-19

- Remember:
  a. A *simple* sentence is a group of words with a complete thought containing a subject and a predicate.
  b. A *compound* sentence contains 2 or more simple sentences.
  c. A *complex* sentence contains one independent clause and one or more dependent (subordinate) clauses.
  d. A *compound-complex* sentence contains a compound sentence with a complex sentence.

LESSON 21-I SENTENCE ERRORS

There are several common sentence errors that are made in writing.

1. Sentence fragment

A fragment is an incomplete sentence. Either a subject or a predicate is missing, or the complete thought of the sentence is omitted.

Examples:

a. Rejoicing in the Lord. (Who is rejoicing?)

b. While I was singing. (What happened while the person was singing? The thought is incomplete.)

2. Comma fault

Another serious kind of error is the comma fault. This happens when two sentences that should have been separated by a semicolon or a period are joined together by a comma.

Examples:

(Incorrect) John the Baptist's mother was Elizabeth, his father was Zacharias.

(Correct) John the Baptist's mother was Elizabeth; his father was Zacharias.

(Correct) John the Baptist's mother was Elizabeth. His father was Zacharias.

3. Run-on Sentence

The run-on sentence is a serious type of sentence error. Continuing from one sentence to another sentence without informing the reader when one sentence ends is a run-on sentence.

Example:

(Incorrect) John the Baptist baptized Jesus John bare record, saying, I saw the Spirit descending from heaven like a dove it abode upon him.

Corrected forms

a. John the Baptist baptized Jesus. John bare recored, saying, I saw the Spirit descending from heaven like a dove. It abode upon him.

b. John the Baptist baptized Jesus. John bare record, saying, I saw the Spirit descending from heaven like a dove, and it abode upon him.

EXPLORING TRUTHS

Read Matthew 28 which contains the glorious resurrection story. Find one verse which contains a subordinate clause. Copy this verse on a sheet of paper and use it as a topic sentence. Then write a paragraph developing the sentence with facts from the book of Matthew.

FINAL TEST ON PART IV

Study the following sentences and in the space at the right tell whether the sentence is a simple sentence, a compound sentence, a complex sentence, a compound-complex sentence. If the sentence is a complex sentence, tell what kind of a subordinate clause is included in it.

1. Now at the feast the governor was wont to release unto the people a prisoner, whom they would. ____________
2. And they had then a notable prisoner, called Barabbas. ____________
3. For he knew that for envy they had delivered him. ____________
4. When Pilate saw that he could prevail nothing, but that rather a tumult was made, he took water, and washed his hands before the multitude, saying, I am innocent of the blood of this just person; see ye to it. ____________
5. Then released he Barabbas unto them. ____________
6. Then the soldiers of the governor took Jesus into the common hall and gathered unto him the whole band of soldiers. ____________
7. And they stripped him and put on him a scarlet robe. ____________
8. And when they had platted a crown of thorns, they put it upon his head, and a reed in his right hand, and they bowed the knee before him, and mocked him, saying, Hail, King of the Jews! ____________
9. They spit upon him, and they took the reed and smote him on the head. ____________
10. They mocked him; they took the robe off from him; they led him away to be crucified. ____________

from Matthew 27:15-31

Final Test

Read the following passage. Complete the test placed at the end of the passage.

ACTS 2:22-38

Ye men of Israel, hear these words; Jesus of Nazareth, [1] a man approved of God among you by miracles and wonders and signs, which God did by him in the midst of you, as ye [2] yourselves also know: Him, being delivered by the determinate counsel and foreknowledge of God, ye have taken, and by [3] wicked hands have crucified and slain: [4] Whom God hath raised up, having loosed the pains of death: because it was not possible that he should be holden of it.

For David speaketh concerning him, I [5] foresaw the Lord always before my face; for he is on my right hand, that I should not be moved: Therefore did my heart rejoice, and my tongue was [6] glad; moreover also my flesh shall rest in hope: Because thou wilt not leave my soul in hell, neither wilt thou suffer thine Holy One [7] to see corruption.

Thou hast made known to me the ways of life; thou shalt make me [8] full of joy with thy countenance.

[9] Men and brethren, let me [10] freely speak unto you of the patriarch David, [11] that he is both dead and buried, and his sepulchre is with us unto this day.

Therefore being a prophet, and knowing that God had sworn [12] with an oath to him, that of the [13] fruit of his loins, according to the flesh, he would raise up Christ to sit on his throne;

He, [14] seeing this before, spake of the resurrection of Christ, that his soul was not left in hell, neither his flesh did see [15] corruption.

This Jesus hath [16] God raised up, whereof we all are [17] witnesses.

Therefore being by the right hand of God exalted, and having received of the Father the promise of the Holy Ghost, he hath shed forth [18] this, which ye now see and hear.

For David is not ascended into the heavens: but he saith himself, The Lord said unto my Lord, Sit thou on my right hand, Until I make thy foes thy footstool.

Therefore let all the house of Israel know assuredly, [19] that God hath made that same Jesus, whom ye have crucified, [20] both Lord and Christ.

Now [21] when they heard this, they [22] were pricked in their heart, and said unto Peter and to the rest of the apostles, Men and brethren, [23] what shall we do?

Then Peter said unto them, Repent, and be baptized every [24] one of you in the name [25] of Jesus Christ for the remission of sins, and ye [26] shall receive the gift of the Holy Ghost.

From the above passage find an example of each of the grammatical expressions listed below. Place the number given above the underlined words, phrases, and clauses next to the appropriate grammatical term. The first one has been done for you.

Answers

16 1. subject of a sentence
_______ 2. adverbial prepositional phrase
_______ 3. appositive phrase
_______ 4. adjective clause
_______ 5. direct object
_______ 6. verb in the passive voice
_______ 7. verb in the active voice
_______ 8. objective complement
_______ 9. proper noun
_______ 10. adjective
_______ 11. participial phrase
_______ 12. infinitive
_______ 13. noun clause
_______ 14. predicate adjective
_______ 15. noun of direct address
_______ 16. object of a preposition
_______ 17. adverb
_______ 18. intensive pronoun
_______ 19. adjective prepositional phrase
_______ 20. adverbial clause
_______ 21. predicate noun
_______ 22. relative pronoun
_______ 23. verb in the future tense
_______ 24. interrogative pronoun
_______ 25. indefinite pronoun
_______ 26. demonstrative pronoun

Printed in the United States
1318000003B/9-10

Made in the USA
Middletown, DE
08 December 2023